MAKING MONEY WHILE MAKING A DIFFERENCE

Also by Richard Steckel:

Filthy Rich & Other Nonprofit Fantasies:
Changing the Way Nonprofits Do Business in the 90s
(with Robin Simons & Peter Lengsfelder)

In Search of America's Best Nonprofits
(with Jennifer Lehman)

MAKING MONEY WHILE

MAKING A DIFFERENCE

How to Profit with a Nonprofit Partner

Richard Steckel, Ph.D., Robin Simons,

Jeffrey Simons, and Norman Tanen

HIGH TIDE PRESS › 1999

A HIGH TIDE BOOK
Published by High Tide Press Inc.
3650 West 183rd Street, Homewood, Illinois 60430
www.hightidepress.com / toll-free: 1-888-487-7377

"Kurt Aschermann's 10 Commandments for Cause-Related Marketing" reprinted courtesy of *Corporate Philanthropy Report*, published by Aspen Publishers Inc. (800-655-5597).

Portions of this book were originally published in Doing best by doing good: How to use public-purpose partnerships to boost corporate profits and benefit your community, *by Richard Steckel and Robin Simons, published by Dutton, 1992, (ISBN 0-525-93490-1).*

Library of Congress Catalog Card Number: 99-71802
Steckel, Richard; Simons, Robin; Simons, Jeffrey; Tanen, Norman. Making money while making a difference: How to profit with a nonprofit partner / by Richard Steckel, Robin Simons, Jeffrey Simons, and Norman Tanen. Includes Bibliography and Index. Revised ed.

ISBN 0-9653744-9-1

Cover design by June Fernandez
Book design by Alex Lubertozzi

Printed in the United States of America
04 03 02 01 00   6 5 4 3 2

Revised Edition

Printed on acid-free paper. ∞

*To the growing number of social entrepreneurs
who add to the inspiring examples of successful strategic alliances
between for-profit corporations and nonprofit organizations.*

CONTENTS

Part III > A Nonprofit Primer

Part IV > How to Engage in Successful Strategic Alliances

MAKING MONEY WHILE MAKING A DIFFERENCE

This is a hell of a story.

It's about a group of young, idealistic people who stopped a war, cleaned up a planet, and pursued equality with passion. They redefined what power was, taking it out of the hands of the people in charge and putting it into the hands of the people who weren't.

Then they grew up.

They became movers and shakers and doers and makers, and overnight they turned into the people they'd spent their lives struggling against. They grew rich and powerful and forgot for a time what they believed when they were young.

Now they stand on the threshold of possibility, a little older, a little wiser. They stand looking out over a world they'd set out to change—only now, they have the real power to change it. They've been joined on the ledge by a younger generation, eager to make their own difference, and just as capable of doing so.

Some of them have already begun changing the world.

This is their story, and by the end of it, maybe it will be yours, too.

>   >   >   >

Think of this book as an *Anarchist Cookbook* for the new millennium. Or *Zen and the Art of Corporate Maintenance*. This book is filled with the stories of heroes who are using their power in corporate America to change the world, while still succeeding at business. Big companies like American Express and smaller companies like Ben & Jerry's. Old companies like Johnson & Johnson and new companies like Timberland. Heroes like Anita Roddick and Paul Newman and Jerry Welsh.

We're not talking altruism here. We're talking about making money. This book is filled with tools you can use to increase your company's profits while making the world a better place. Example after example of methods of lowering costs, increasing sales, improving employee morale and retention, building consumer loyalty and company image. All of these examples fit under the umbrella of "strategic corporate citizenship."

The idea behind strategic corporate citizenship—which includes strategic alliances and cause-related marketing (CRM)—is that there are areas of common interest between nonprofits and business. Find the right one, the one that benefits both parties, that does good, that is honest, and everyone profits. And when we say profits, we don't mean goody-two-shoes profits, but honest-to-goodness, bottom-line-boosting, stock-price-lifting, real profits.

Nonprofit corporations are, for the most part, unsung heroes taking on more than their fair share of the really hard problems in the world: hunger, child abuse, disease, education, rehabilitation... the list is endless.

Nonprofit corporations have a problem. Nobody wants to pay for their products. For example, everyone is in favor of ending hunger. Maybe if we could go to a store and buy it in a can, we would. Because the solution isn't that easy, we tend to do nothing. We send them a $25 check or buy some cookies at a fundraiser, and we pat ourselves on the back and say we helped.

It doesn't have to be that way.

What if society could harness the vast power of corporate America and use it to effect social change? Even better, what if doing so could also increase corporate profits?

It can.

This book is filled with examples of companies of every size working with nonprofits of every type to gain all sorts of benefits. Some of the examples stretch back to the dawn of cause-related marketing, way back in 1983. And some of them are so new that the results of the programs aren't known yet. Since strategic alliances are still evolving, we thought it important to show you any innovation, from the first ground-breaking efforts to the latest new wrinkle.

If we wanted to be totally mercenary, we could call this book *What's In It For You?* There are so many benefits to getting involved with a nonprofit the right way, that this could sound like a slick sales pitch.

It's not. We've got real world examples proving these methods work.

And that's good news. Because late at night, when you've dragged yourself home from another killer day at the office fighting not to violate your ethics or destroy what's left of your integrity, don't you dream of a world in which you can do your job well and still do what's right?

When you were younger you said, "When I'm in charge, I'm going to do it better. It's not just going to be about money, it's going to be about doing what's right."

Guess what? You are in charge now. In charge of advertising budgets. In charge of vendor selection. In charge of sales. In charge of human resources. Some of you have done really well, and are in charge of the whole show.

So now is the time. This book is going to show you how you can increase your profitability by spending your money in the right places. American Express does. Reebok does. Apple does. Johnson & Johnson does. And they do it with nonprofit partners that range from the American Cancer Society to *Sesame Street.*

You *can* make money while making a difference. And you know the best part? You'll feel really good while you do it. And how often does that happen at work these days?

Remember how good it felt to change the world? Well, it's time to do it again.

A Little About Nonprofits

First of all, a short course in what nonprofits are, so you can see why they're such good partners. Part III of this book goes into more detail about what nonprofits are and how to deal with them. But just in case you're not sure about these strange, seemingly anti-business businesses, let's give you a quick description.

The nonprofit sector is made up of around 1.4 million organizations, with operating expenditures of $500 billion. It includes nearly half our hospitals, most of our civic organizations, 60 percent of our social service agencies, almost all of our symphony orchestras, and about half of our colleges and universities. In fact, the first nonprofit corporation in America was Harvard College, established in the mid 1600s.

The primary mission of a corporation is to make profit. The mission of a nonprofit corporation is to make the world a better place. Nothing says a corporation can't save the world also, as long as it makes a profit to keep its shareholders and board of directors happy. Nonprofits, on the other hand, are prohibited from making a profit by the IRS, in return for which they don't have to pay taxes on their income... well, sort of. The tax code that governs earned income by nonprofits specifies three characteristics an activity must meet in order to be taxable (or avoid in order to remain non-taxable):

1. It must be "unrelated to the organization's tax-exempt mission."
2. It must be "regularly carried on."
3. It must be deemed a "trade or business."

In other words, as long as a nonprofit engages in an activity related to its mission, it is allowed to earn income from that activity to pay for expenses, salaries, programs, and other things that allow it to do its job in the world. It's allowed to accept volunteers, merchandise, and donations. It's allowed to produce products and sell them above cost. When done right, it's not only possible to earn large amounts of money, it's also absolutely legal and ethical.

The benefits to a nonprofit for engaging in strategic alliances are tremendous: increased operating income, increased visibility, a diversified income base, increased experience and reinforcement of business skills. Strategic alliances are very much a two-way street in which both parties can derive benefits they couldn't get anywhere else.

> > > >

Part I of this book tells you everything you need to know about why now is the time to pursue strategic alliances.

Part II of this book explores the major forms of strategic alliances, including cause-related marketing, so you can figure out which ones might be useful to you and your company.

Part III tells you everything you need to know about working with nonprofits in putting together a strategic alliance campaign.

And Part IV puts it all together, taking you through implementing your own strategic alliance, step by step.

Ready? Then let's get started.

PART I

STRATEGIC ALLIANCES:
CAUSE-RELATED MARKETING

1

WHY ENGAGE IN CAUSE-RELATED MARKETING?

"Eighty-four percent [of women] are more receptive to products associated with a cause they care about; affluent, educated women are the most responsive group."

—*Working Woman, May 1997*

<   <   <   <

We all know that the bottom line of business is profit. No matter how altruistic a company may look, when push comes to shove what really counts is money. Cause-related marketing, a term once used to describe all kinds of strategic corporate citizenship, is defined here as a corporate-nonprofit partnership formed to market a product or service for mutual benefit. As you will see, CRM can increase a corporation's profitability in a wide variety of areas.

Companies that associate closely with nonprofits—that genuinely adopt a nonprofit's cause, that measurably help its work—find that something interesting happens. The nonprofit's good will rubs off on them. Nonprofits devote themselves to the public good. So if a nonprofit works with a corporation, people figure the company is on the up and up. People who like the cause look at the company in a new light. They buy products that help the cause they support. Even public perception can change—people begin to see the company as one that cares about issues as well as profits. In May 1997, *Time* reported on a 1996 Cone/Roper survey finding that "76 percent of consumers would switch to a corporate brand or product that supports worthy causes; provided that the price and quality were on par with other goods." The 1999 Cone/Roper survey numbers remain consistently high regarding consumer opinions on cause-related marketing, signaling that these programs are not a passing fad, but rather a must-do for brands striving to increase their relationships with customers, employees, communities, and business partners. "Americans have made it clear over a five-year period that cause-marketing influences their perception of brands and their purchasing decisions," says Brad Fay, senior VP of Roper Starch Worldwide. A consumer survey in New Zealand illustrated that supporting causes makes customers more favorable to particular brands, with children's health, rescue services, local schools, and general health the most positive image enhancers.

In addition to improved perception, cause-related marketing can boost sales and help a company stand out from the crowd. As brand image and consumer loyalty begin to lose some of their importance, as products begin to merge together within the sensory overload of modern multimedia consumer bombardment, a CRM partnership with a good cause can distinguish a company's products and services from the competition. CRM ventures can get a lot of press, so they can also provide a company with a marketing edge.

Finally, CRM partnerships help companies internally. Many employees want to work for a company they can feel proud of. Surveys show that people would rather work in a company that's active in their community. And with qualified employees getting harder to find and even harder to hold on to, partnering with a nonprofit can give a company an edge in hiring and retention.

Pretty impressive, right? Within these categories—image building, marketing, human relations—the list of specific benefits is quite long. CRM campaigns are flexible enough to meet multiple corporate needs. To show you just how flexible, we've collected some pretty impressive examples of how real cause-related marketing benefited real corporations.

Stand Out from the Crowd
Working Assets and Social Activism

In an age of "me-too" advertising, CRM campaigns can help corporations stand out from the pack. The competition may make their products look just like yours in a commercial, but they can't duplicate your CRM venture with a worthy cause. That partnership gives your campaign a personality and a value that can't be matched by conventional ads.

Few fields are as competitive as long distance phone service and credit cards. Working Assets has decided to compete in both industries, and thanks to their unique CRM efforts, in 1997 *Inc.* magazine named them one of the fastest growing companies in the nation for the fifth year in a row. To what do they owe their success? Working Assets gives one percent of their customers' monthly charges to "nonprofit groups working for peace, equality, human rights, and the environment." Each monthly phone bill acts as an activist newsletter, highlighting two crucial issues under debate. One of the more interesting perks customers receive: free daily phone calls to targeted decision makers in Congress, the White House, and corporate boardrooms. Since they began in 1985, the company has raised over $12 million in donations, $3 million in 1997. Their customer base has grown to include 300,000 residential and 3,000 commercial telephone users and 100,000 credit card holders.

Reinforce Image Advertising
Nabisco Animal Crackers and the World Wildlife Fund

Once you've introduced a theme in your ads, partnership with the right nonprofit can reinforce that theme to consumers. Nabisco's Animal Crackers are one of the best known brands of cookies in the world. Their image was so strong that they hadn't changed their box in ninety years. Could CRM help reinforce a nearly century-old advertising message and energize sales?

When Nabisco entered into a CRM venture with the World Wildlife Fund (WWF), they went wild. They changed the familiar shapes of the cookies to those of various endangered species. They changed the box string to green and included pictures of four animals that were on the endangered species list. They also promised to donate five cents from every sale to the WWF, up to $100,000. The results? Equally wild—a 20 percent sales increase over the course of the two-year promotion.

Increase Consumer Loyalty
Avon, Nivea, and Breast Cancer

The days of "I'd rather fight than switch" are over. Increasingly critical consumers are being offered a wealth of new products, and it's tougher than ever to keep them loyal. Linking your product to a nonprofit cause can reinforce that loyalty. Besides the benefits of association, you can use the nonprofit to create tangible reminders to your buyers of why they're right to do business with you.

Few issues have grabbed the spotlight recently like breast cancer.

According to the 1998 Cone Breast Cancer Awareness Trend Tracker, nearly twenty-six million women purchased a product or service linked to breast cancer awareness during October, National Breast Cancer Awareness Month. The win for supporting breast cancer causes is big, according to the Cone survey. Thirty-three percent of women surveyed are likely to purchase a product or service linked to breast cancer throughout the year. Numbers like this justify the involvement of so many corporations. Revlon spent about $5 million on research in 1996, and since 1993 Estée-Lauder has spent over $2.2 million on Breast Cancer research. In the United Kingdom, Nivea raised £5 million for a hospital devoted to Breast Cancer research and treatment. Nivea engaged in a CRM partnership with Fashion Targets Breast Cancer, a charity supported by models, designers, and members of the fashion industry. The effort has given Nivea an increased appeal to younger women, while improving its visibility in the crowded cosmetics market.

Other most recognized in the Cone Survey include the U.S. Postal Service's Pink Ribbon Stamp Program, the American Cancer Society, and Rosie O'Donnell. JC Penney and Ford Motor Company's sponsorship of "Race for the Cure" and the WNBA Breast Cancer Health Education programs also scored well among women asked about specific programs. But by far, the biggest winner in the survey was Avon.

Avon joined the fight against breast cancer in 1993. By 1999 they had already committed $32 million through cause-related marketing efforts, funding over 250 programs and setting up a Worldwide Fund for Women's Health. In a quest to find one aspect of the issue they could own, Avon chose education and early detection. According to Joanne Mazurki, originally Avon's Breast Cancer Awareness Crusade program director and now director of global cause-related marketing, "We wanted to leverage the strength of the company and make this issue ours. Through its vast direct marketing program, this is a company that can reach people wherever they are."

Has it paid off for Avon? Mazurki says, "Our goal is not direct profit, but the 'halo effect' it gives us. This has improved our relationship not only with customers, but also with our sales organization, and there are two things that drive this business: one, representatives who are proud to work for the company, and two, customers who are happy to let us in the door... Have we quantified the value? No. Do we want to? No. We believe it's the right thing to do."

Avon may not have quantified the value, but the 1998 Cone study did. Avon's Breast Cancer Awareness Crusade was the number one program identified without prompting by the women surveyed.

Attract Media Coverage
Coors' "Literacy: Pass It On"

New + worthy = newsworthy. It's corny, but it's true. And that's the magic of cause-related marketing events. They're new and unusual. They benefit a worthy cause. They catch the eye of the media. CRM ventures with nonprofits often generate far more coverage than you can get on your own. The tie-in with a nonprofit qualifies the event or program for free public service announcements, media placements that would otherwise be prohibitively expensive. Coors found that along with media coverage, intelligently conceived CRM can accomplish multiple goals. Coors' "Literacy: Pass It On" consumer promotion campaign succeeded in attracting media coverage and enhancing Coors' reputation and image to specific markets and the general public.

Over the course of a five-year program, Coors donated nearly $6 million to over 250 local, regional, and national adult literacy organizations. The program exceeded its goal of reaching 500,000 adults with literacy services, and the Coors Literacy Hotline was called approximately 100,000 times.

With nearly two billion media impressions during its first four years, the campaign enhanced Coors' reputation and corporate image to the African American, Hispanic, and Women's markets, as well as the general public. There was significant and positive coverage of Coors' commitment to adult literacy in the media including *ABC News Today Show, Entertainment Tonight, Good Morning America, USA Today,* ABC Radio, *Larry King Live,* Black Entertainment Television, *CBS This Morning,* the *Tonight Show,* the *New York Times, BusinessWeek,* CNN, and TNN News. The program helped forge relationships with legislators, including thirty members of the U.S. Congress from both parties. And Coors won accolades from such diverse sources as the National Puerto Rican Forum, the National Federation of Press Women, the Literacy Volunteers of America, and the Ceba Award of Excellence in Advertising & Communications to the African American Community.

Safeway was one of nearly 200 distributors that joined the five-year long Coors effort. Participating retailers in a five-state area reported as much as a triple-digit sales increase. Display coverage exceeded 95 percent. According to a spokesperson, "It strengthened retail relationships, enhanced our corporate image in the Northwest and resulted in ads, displays, and increased sales." It also resulted in the first Coors product feature in six years.

Safeway wasn't alone. Seven distributors partnered with Lucky's, the largest grocery chain in Southern California, and reported triple-digit, tri-brand sales increases. Osco, a Chicago area distributor, saw a 40 percent sales increase and stronger relationships with 130 retailers.

Reverse Negative Publicity
Texaco and Child Road Safety

The Tylenol tampering scare changed how corporate America dealt with negative publicity. The best defense against negative publicity is a good offense. And one of the best offenses you can use is a CRM venture. The local, targeted, and "wholesome" nature of such campaigns makes them especially effective for this use. A poorly conceived or insincere campaign can backfire, tarnishing the images of the corporation and the nonprofit involved. But a smart campaign can make all the difference in the world.

Texaco UK proved this recently when, faced with negative publicity across a broad range of issues on a worldwide level, they turned to a cause near and dear to every motorist's heart: the safety of their children.

Reports by Gallup Research told Texaco UK that consumers perceived them as a macho company that was out of tune with the 90s, and that public opinion was on a negative trend toward oil companies. Advertising, Sales, and Promotion Manager Richard Little decided it was time to reverse the trend by enhancing Texaco's social image. He decided to support a current initiative by the Department of Transportation to increase awareness about how many children were killed in automobile accidents. Texaco came up with the tag line, "Children should be seen and not hurt." Their advertising followed the government's television presence, supporting the suggestions of the Department of Transportation for improving safety. Texaco delivered 2.5 million government-developed leaflets about child road safety. They distributed posters and made reflective, non-toxic children's clothing stickers available at retail. And 862 company employees volunteered their time to participate in the program.

Did Texaco get what they wanted from their CRM venture? Public opinion showed rapid improvement. Research indicated that in the minds of the public, Texaco owned the tag line, "Children should be seen and not hurt." But most important, that line now meant something as a result of Texaco's efforts. By the end of the second quarter of the program, pedestrian and cycling casualties were down 22 percent. Texaco had reversed their sliding public opinion by doing something unusual for an oil company—they earned the public's respect.

Facilitate Market Entry
Nortel and Developing Countries

Looking to break into a new market? Tie in with a local nonprofit or cause. Helping a community with an issue it cares about can be the fastest way to establish your name and reputation. Choosing an area that your company logically relates to seems like a natural connection, not an insincere one.

Sometimes you have to build a market before you can enter it. That's what Nortel, an international telecommunications firm, had to do before it could expand operations into the potentially lucrative markets represented by emerging nations. Because developing nations lacked access to technologies for reducing chlorofluorocarbons (CFCs), Nortel facilitated the transfer of their own technologies to local companies. Nortel forged a relationship with the Industry Cooperative for Ozone Layer Protection and the World Bank. Using their own personnel in joint ventures and partnerships, they trained companies in Mexico, Brazil, Vietnam, Turkey, and China in the reduction of ozone-destroying CFCs. As a result of this demonstration of environmental leadership combined with the cascading effect of knowledge transfer, Nortel has built an excellent reputation and image in the markets it was trying to enter. Local media responded with positive coverage. During the course of these programs, Nortel established valuable contacts with potential suppliers, customers, and officials. Nortel's efforts made it easier for them to enter new markets, and saved them millions on CFC reduction and disposal when they did.

Improve Employee Retention, Recruitment, and Morale
Dow and the Wildlife Habitat Enhancement Council

In the same way that CRM campaigns can be used to entertain clients, they can also provide opportunities to reward employees with perks. Free or discounted tickets, special admissions, private classes, exclusive parties, chances to meet celebrities, and other benefits are usually easy to design into CRM promotions. All of these boost employees' loyalty and reward them for their service.

You're not the only one who wants to use your energy to make the world a better place; your employees do, too. Over a decade ago, David Lewin at the UCLA Institute of Industrial Relations studied 188 companies in 1987 and 1989 and found that employee morale was three times higher in companies with a strong degree of community involvement. More recently, a 1996 study in Britain conducted by MORI, a British market research firm, found similar results.

We shouldn't be surprised. Most people want to feel good about the place they work. In an age filled with problems, employees want to feel that their companies are forging solutions, not making things worse. And people love the opportunity to help. For these reasons, companies are increasingly encouraging employees to volunteer. Employee volunteering is the fastest-growing aspect of cause-related marketing. It stretches the corporate donation, boosts employee morale, and gives much-needed help to the nonprofit cause.

Dow Chemical Company encourages its employees to volunteer in a partnership program with the Wildlife Habitat Enhancement Council (WHEC) to preserve and restore wildlife habitats on Dow's corporate property. The company owns 860 acres near Joliet, Illinois, that contain wetlands, woodlands, and grasslands. With the help of WHEC, Dow employees build nesting boxes, conduct controlled burns, and provide other needed labor to restore the property to habitat condition. Given some of the negative publicity that has been directed at the chemical industry, this allows employees an opportunity to preserve the environment and feel better about their jobs.

2

WHY ENGAGE IN STRATEGIC CORPORATE CITIZENSHIP?

"Marketers need to stand out from the crowd. Offering a connection to a good cause is an increasingly effective way to do that."

—*Bradford Fay*
Senior VP
Roper Starch Worldwide

< < < <

Why engage in strategic corporate citizenship?

It's tempting to answer, "Because we can."

It's probably more accurate to say, "Because we must."

We must for two reasons. Business has changed, with a changing workforce that has different requirements and expectations, increased advertising clutter and competition on a local and worldwide scale, and an aggressive consumer marketplace that demands more socially responsible actions from business. The second reason is that the nonprofit sector has changed. Cutbacks in government funding mean the nonprofit sector needs more help than it has ever needed before. With more entrepreneurial nonprofits than ever, the sector is willing and able to pull its own weight. But to do that it needs strategic alliances with for-profit corporations.

This chapter (and the next) will offer reasons that answer the question, Why now? From the overwhelming deluge of advertising clutter to the unprecedented call for volunteerism by four American presidents, the benefits of strategic corporate citizenship will become clear.

Challenge #1: The Changing Workforce

Want to talk change? Let's talk about the workforce, an area in which every "given," every expectation, every formula by which business used to operate is radically different from what it was a decade ago, or a decade before that.

Two decades ago, workers were a dime a dozen. There were millions of baby boomers who came from nice suburban homes, went to nice suburban schools. They took a job and did it, few questions asked, few demands made.

The 90s saw a radical shift in the workforce. Today's workforce is a different story. Tomorrow's will be like no other in American history. Baby boomers will retire by the millions, being replaced by younger workers. Of those new workers, more are women and minorities than ever before.

What does this mean for business? As these new workers join the labor pool, they bring a whole new set of needs and demands, previously unfelt in corporations:

> > With more working women comes increased concern over the needs of the family: already companies are offering child care, elder care, flexible time, and flexible benefits for helping employees deal with family concerns. Since Home Depot instituted their "Our Babies and You" program, it has decreased premature births and defects among the infants of their associates and lowered company health care expenses dramatically. "The primary reason we began our prenatal program is because of its ability to be an employee relations tool. The associates love it," says Wes Lecroy, Home Depot's wellness coordinator.

> > Minorities require different management styles: already companies are instituting training programs to help employees of different ethnic groups communicate.

> > Immigrants require language accommodations: at Digital Equipment Corporation's Boston plant, employees speak nineteen languages. Company announcements are printed in English, Chinese, French, Spanish, Portuguese, Vietnamese, and Haitian Creole.

As the number of unskilled, uneducated workers grows, skilled workers are becoming more valuable. Companies are finding they must work harder to attract and retain them, since these desirable workers also place new demands on their employers. The good news is that companies that address these concerns have discovered some unexpected benefits. The major concerns break down into three main categories:

Family First > Having delayed marriage and family for their careers, many workers are now making up for lost time. They are leaving jobs that demand long hours, opting for part-time jobs and job-sharing. They are requesting flexible schedules that permit them to visit their children's teachers, take vacations, and attend school plays. They are demanding flexible benefit packages that help them meet family needs.

Meaning On the Job > Today's skilled workers don't want jobs, they want careers. They want to be listened to and trusted. They want the freedom to make decisions. They want flexibility and creativity, room to contribute, and room to grow.

Meaning In the Job > Current workers want to be part of companies they believe in. They want to feel that their company is contributing solutions to the problems facing the world. In a 1996 study of employees at Gillette and Polaroid conducted by the Center for Corporate Community Relations at Boston College, 84 percent of employees believe a company's image in the community is important. The study found that employees who feel their company has a strong community presence also feel loyal to the company, and positive about themselves. These numbers are closely reflected by a 1996 British MORI survey in which 86 percent of respondents agreed that a company that supports society and the community is probably a good company to work for.

Can business rise to the challenges of the new workforce? Successful enterprises will—by developing flexible management systems, by encouraging problem-solving and autonomy, by strengthening their communities to increase the pool of skilled employees, and by engaging in socially responsible behavior that attracts desirable workers. Strategic alliances are one vehicle that will help companies respond to these human resource needs.

Challenge #2: The Rise of Niche Marketing and Advertising Clutter

In the good old days, when growth was the buzzword and new consumers were easy to find, mass marketing was a perfectly respectable—and reasonably efficient—way to expand market share. Companies offered products and services to broad market segments. By advertising on network TV, in mass-market magazines, and in daily newspapers, they could be fairly well assured that enough consumers would see their ads, want their products, and respond. Today this broad market strategy no longer works. In addition, increasingly sophisticated consumers are demanding ever more specialized products. As a result, the sheer number of products has increased, but the market for each has become smaller and more specialized. Mass-market vehicles are now too expensive and reach too many of the "wrong" consumers to justify their cost.

Advertising clutter has also made it more difficult for a company to get its message heard. With thirty-two hundred advertising messages bombarding consumers each day, how can you ensure that they'll hear yours?

How can companies market successfully in this climate? Strategic alliances can help by enabling companies to "micro-market": to reach small groups of consumers with similar needs and wants. Strategic partnerships can help companies differentiate their products and services from the competition's by building strong associations between products and nonprofit causes. And they can help companies build long-term relationships with customers by promoting companies' long-term commitments to a cause.

Challenge #3: The Changing Role of Government

This is a challenge that, on the surface, more directly affects nonprofits than it does corporations. But when you look deeper, it really affects everybody. Let's look at what happened and why it's such an opportunity for business.

The Republican Revolution rolled into Washington on promises of reducing government spending, in areas that include entitlements and other forms of social spending. The Republicans believe that if those programs were important, the free market system would pick up the slack. (We don't disagree with this premise, by the way. This book is about showing business why it's profitable to pick up that slack, and how to do it.)

The budget resolution passed by Congress in 1996 called for a cumulative reduction of 18 percent of federal support for nonprofits over the years 1997-2002. This works out to $90 billion of lost government funding to hospitals, colleges, universities, social service agencies, civic organizations, and the arts. We're not even addressing changes in the way the government taxes nonprofits, which may result in even larger operating deficits.

No matter what any government spin-doctor says, $90 billion is a lot of money. Welfare programs have been cut. Housing subsidies have declined. Eligibility for Medicaid has been tightened. In areas in which government funds have remained stable, hardships have mounted, causing a net loss in support. The resulting problems are all too familiar: increasing poverty and homelessness, deteriorating infrastructures, failing school and healthcare systems, rising devastation by drugs and crime.

In an effort to stem the loss of services, government is asking business to take up the slack. As Tommy Thompson, Governor of Wisconsin, said, "I would go in and start saying that businesses have got to be our partner. They've got to start shouldering some of the responsibility."

America isn't the only government turning to industry for help. In April 1998 Australian Prime Minister John Howard held the first meeting of the Government's business and community roundtable. He told the meeting that people were looking for "a new balance between government, business, and the community."

Business is responding to the challenge. It is venturing into issues such as education, substance abuse, and AIDS care and education by supporting workplace and community programs. It is contracting with federal and state agencies to perform government functions, such as operating prisons, providing mail service, and collecting garbage. It is forming partnerships with nonprofit agencies to strengthen communities through job training programs and economic development. It is hiring tens of thousands under the Welfare-to-Work programs.

The cutback in government services has created a new role for business. There's a government-sponsored "fire sale" on good works and community involvement taking place. But can business afford to buy?

Enlightened companies believe they have no choice. They know that investment in schools will produce qualified employees. They know that investment in the arts will help make communities better places to live and work. They know that investment in social services will help keep the United States competitive.

The numbers support their premise, at least in the United Kingdom. In 1993 Ernst and Young figured out that the cost of the failing educational system in terms of crime and lost markets amounted to £8.3 billion every year. By now that number is considerably higher.

That's the "socially-responsible" reason to get involved. As we've shown in other parts of this book, there's a mercenary side, too. Every opportunity to unite with a good cause, in whatever form is most appropriate, gives a company a competitive edge.

The old strategies, the old ways of thinking and operating just don't work anymore. Whereas once upon a time a business was responsible primarily to stockholders, today a business is responsible to stakeholders—the customers, employees, suppliers, shareholders, the government, the neighborhood, the environment—to all the people and places that business affects.

It's a tall order for a company that just wants to make and sell its widgets. But companies that fail to fill that order won't survive. Companies that want to fill the order will find strategic partnerships with nonprofits a powerful instrument for building long-term profitability and survival.

There's still one more answer to the question, Why engage in strategic corporate citizenship? It's a big one—big enough that it gets its own chapter. After all, anything that can not only bring together President Clinton, former presidents Bush, Carter and Ford, Nancy Reagan, and General Colin Powell deserves its own chapter.

3

DO THE RIGHT THING OR ELSE!

"What I want to see us do is to elevate the good practices that are going on, show how they are consistent with making money and succeeding in the free enterprise system, and hope we can reinforce that kind of conduct that many of you have brought to bear in your own companies and with your own employees."

—Bill Clinton
White House Conference on Corporate Citizenship
March 1996

"We have to do in the world what we spent the better part of this century doing here at home—we have got to put a human face on the global economy."

—Bill Clinton
State of The Union Address
January 1999

<   <   <   <

President Clinton gets it—and recognizes that business gets it too. Long before the White House Conference on Corporate Citizenship in 1996, or the President's Summit for America's Future in 1997, corporate America began improving its level of citizenship.

It had to. Business was being held more accountable for its practices than ever before. When companies failed their citizenship duties, as in Union Carbide's plant disaster in Bophal, India, the Exxon Valdez oil spill, and Texaco's employee discrimination, the impact on the stock's value and costs were dramatic. The response from angry consumers can lead to corporate mailboxes filled with shredded credit cards, in Exxon's case. Or rotting food, in the case of the world's largest fast-food company, McDonald's. Many claim that McDonald's shifted from Styrofoam food containers to paper after their offices were inundated with used Big Mac packages.

In Europe, consumer disapproval can turn violent. When Greenpeace drummed up protests against Shell UK's environmentally-challenged plan to dispose of a used oil rig in the ocean, boycotts in Germany cut sales in half, fifty Shell stations were vandalized, two fire-bombed, and one raked with bullets, while employee morale plummeted. On top of all this, it cost Shell $200 million to change their oil rig disposal decision.

Why are consumers responding to corporations with the same zeal and venom they turned against governments in the 60s? Perhaps because, as a 1996 *BusinessWeek*/Harris Poll concluded, 71 percent of Americans say business has too much power and is morally responsible for the country's woes. The poll pointed out that 95 percent of adults rejected the view that a corporation's only role is to make money. And that 95 percent of Americans believe companies owe responsibility to communities and employees, as well as to stockholders.

Or perhaps the consumers are getting restless because many multinational corporations are as powerful as—or even more powerful than—many countries. In the mid 90s, there were only nineteen countries whose GNP was larger than the worth of General Motors. According to *The Economist's Yearbook* for 1997, "Draw up a list of the world's largest 100 economies in 1997 and fifty will turn out to be corporations. General Motors' sales revenues will roughly equal the combined GNP of Tanzania, Ethiopia, Nepal, Bangladesh, Zaire, Uganda, Nigeria, Kenya, and Pakistan." Even governments are concerned. A British Cabinet Minister recently told Bill Gates of Microsoft, "People like you are reducing my power to govern."

Here's what Cor Herkstroter, worldwide head of Shell, had to say about it: "In the past few years, Shell, like many other multinationals, has faced some very complex dilemmas... We were perhaps excessively focused on internal matters and we failed to fully understand the need to provide information to the general public...We were seen as unresponsive, and so, to some extent, became targets... we were somewhat slow in understanding that these groups (environmentalist, consumer) were tending to acquire authority. Meanwhile those institutions we were used to dealing with (government, industry) were

tending to lose authority. We underestimated the extent of these changes—
we failed to engage in a serious dialogue with these new groups."

Like the protests of the 60s, increased activism is having an impact. The
tuna boycott led to dolphin-safe tuna. Consumer anger forced companies to
stop producing products with chlorofluorocarbons. Now the activism is
spilling over into the courts and the financial markets.

Community activists in Boston forced Fleet Financial to contribute $20
million to the inner city to atone for lending violations. A uranium processing plant lost a $78 million settlement against a Cincinnati neighborhood.
When Texaco was sued for racial discrimination and lost, the settlement was
$176 million. Bausch & Lomb earnings fell 54 percent in 1994 when man-
agers "played fast and loose with accounting principles and ethics." In
October 1996 agricultural giant Archer Daniels Midland (ADM) paid a $100
million fine for price fixing, the largest criminal antitrust fine in history.
Banker's Trust, Pain Webber, Metropolitan Life, Prudential, and John
Hancock have all faced lawsuits and/or fines for questionable practices.
Mercury Finance's stock lost $2.2 billion in the blink of an eye when it was
discovered that they'd been overstating profits for nearly four years.

Boycotts, lawsuits, increased costs, and a whole slew of surveys are sending
a wake-up call to companies around the world.

In the UK the 1996 MORI Annual Survey of Corporate Social
Responsibility reflects increasing consumer demand for corporate responsibility:

> 66 percent say that industry and commerce do not pay enough atten-
   tion to their social responsibilities.

> 82 percent say a company's activities in society and the community
   are important in forming an opinion about that company (34 percent say very important, 48 percent say fairly important).

A strong reputation is critical for organizations that plan to enter the
twenty-first century in a leadership position, according to a 1994 Walker
Research national study on corporate and social responsibility—especially in
highly competitive industries where quality, price, and service are not differ-

entiating factors. In addition, the study found that customers' opinions regarding the company's social responsibility play a large part in purchasing decisions:

> 92 percent of consumers indicate they would be somewhat or much less likely to buy from a company that is not socially responsible (57 percent said they would be *much* less likely to buy).

> 88 percent of consumers indicate that they would be somewhat or much more likely to buy from a company that is a good corporate citizen if the quality, service, and price are equal to that of the competitors (47 percent said they would be *much* more likely to buy).

> Even more interesting is the growing subgroup (16 percent) who reported that they actively sought information about a business' practices before purchasing.

A more recent study is the 1999 Cone/Roper Study (an update of the 1996 study), conducted by Roper Starch Worldwide and Cone/Coughlin Communications, that studied consumer awareness and attitudes toward cause-related marketing and found that:

> 83 percent of consumers report having a more positive image of a company that is doing something to make the world a better place.

> 79 percent of "Influential Americans" report that they would not only switch brands, but also retailers, to support a cause.

> 66 percent of consumers (up from 31 percent) say that when price and quality are equal, a company's responsible business practices are an important factor in deciding whether to buy a brand or not. A company's social responsibility record wins out over a brand's advertising influence in the second tier of purchase factors.

> 66 percent of consumers believe that cause-related marketing is an

acceptable business practice; 61 percent believe it should be a standard part of a company's activities.

These trends are not occurring only in the United States. In fact, some of these surprising numbers are surpassed in the United Kingdom and Australia. In 1996, a British consumer survey by Business in the Community found:

> 86 percent said they would have a more positive image of the company if it were supporting a cause they cared about.

> 80 percent would be willing to change their purchase behavior if they believe doing so would benefit a cause or issue they're concerned about.

> 86 percent are more likely to buy a product associated with a cause or issue.

> 63 percent of consumers feel CRM was an acceptable means of business addressing society's "causes" and issues.

> 64 percent said CRM should be a standard part of a company's activities.

An equivalent survey in Australia by research firm Worthington Di Marzio in 1997 found:

> 49 percent would vote with their wallets and switch brands on the basis of a worthy cause.

> 88 percent expressed a desire to see companies promote their good work with community causes. (Interestingly enough, 23 percent said advertising the CRM is the best proof of a company's commitment to a cause.)

> 83 percent said Australian companies should be involved in CRM.

> 59 percent said CRM should be a standard part of a company's philosophy.

These recent surveys are just the latest of many prophetic voices.

As far back as 1989, the nonprofit Council on Economic Priorities first published *Shopping for a Better World*. It rates 1,300 companies according to social criteria (including charitable giving, advancement of women and minorities, military contracts, environmental policies, and animal testing). According to research conducted by the Council, nearly 70 percent of the book's readers report changing their buying habits based on the book's ratings.

In 1990, a survey by Century Research found that 25 percent of New Yorkers surveyed had stopped buying the products of at least one company because they believed the company wasn't a good environmental citizen.

Perhaps even more disconcerting is the fact that many consumers don't merely switch brands, but are willing to take direct action against corporations that engage in illegal or immoral practices. A recent survey in the United Kingdom reported that two-thirds of the population were more likely to take some sort of action against a company than ten years ago. But it's the kind of action they might take that's alarming. Take a look at these numbers from the poll conducted by the British advertising agency GGT and reported in the *Evening Standard*:

> 60 percent say breaking the law is an acceptable form of protest against business practices they disapprove of.

> 53 percent of those interviewed who are over 55 years old say that breaking the law is justified to show disapproval of corporate behavior.

> 65 percent are more likely to take real action against a company than five years ago.

> 55 percent would stop dealing with a company if they disapproved of its ethics.

Of course, the flip side to these numbers is that if you do the right thing, consumers are willing to pay even more for your product or service. In the Cone/Roper poll, 52 percent would pay 10 percent more for a socially responsible product.

It actually pays to do the right thing.

Other Benefits of Strategic Corporate Citizenship

At the White House Conference on Corporate Citizenship in 1996, President Clinton and representatives from small businesses and large corporations described the business benefits resulting from the integration of social responsibility into corporate strategies.

According to a 1995 report released by Ernst & Young's Center for Business Innovation (commissioned by the Department of Labor) companies that invest in innovative workplace practices are more profitable than those that don't.

The President had plenty of examples to support his point. Examples like Patagonia, Motorola, Starbuck's Coffee, and Marriott International:

> Treating your employees like family has paid off for Patagonia, a maker of outdoor clothing and equipment. Yvon Chouinard, Patagonia's CEO, described the company's family-friendly workplace practices as resulting in significant savings in hiring and training costs. While the average turnover rate for that industry is 20 to 25 percent, it's 4.5 percent at Patagonia's main offices.

> Motorola understands the benefit of commitment to its employees' future. In 1995, they invested $200 million (over three percent of its payroll budget) to educate its workforce. By giving employees new opportunities for advancement and increasing their long-term employability, Motorola gained an estimated $30 in productivity for every one dollar spent.

> Just a few years ago, nobody who hadn't been to the Pacific Northwest had even heard of Starbuck's Coffee. Now, the company enjoys an average growth of 60 percent per year, and there are

Starbuck's springing up everywhere. But rapid expansion brought Starbuck's a problem: keeping those stores staffed with experienced workers. 62 percent of their workforce is part-time, and the attrition rate for the retail and restaurant industry can be up to 400 percent, To staunch this hemorrhage, Chairman and CEO Howard Shultz set out to link shareholder value and the customer experience to employee compensation. Starbuck's comprehensive benefits plan features medical coverage and stock options for all employees. The amazing result: employee attrition at Starbuck's is less than 55 percent.

> Marriott International employs more than 100,000 low-wage workers in its hotels around the world. Some of them came out of the "Pathways to Independence" program. Under the program, welfare recipients undergo dozens of hours of intensive training to prepare them for employment. Once they graduate, they can go on to work for Marriott. Since 1991, 750 people moved from welfare, through the Pathways to Independence program, to jobs at Marriott. More than 300 of them still worked there as of December 1997. In addition, Marriott instituted the Associate Resource Line (ARL), a twenty-four-hour, toll-free telephone counseling and support service to assist employees in dealing with issues of child care, immigration and naturalization, domestic violence, and substance abuse, among others. Did Marriott profit from their socially responsible investment in their people? The company reports a four-to-one payback in reduced absenteeism and tardiness and improved retention, as well as improved customer service. Marriott even received federal tax incentives for hiring welfare recipients.

The President's next recognition of groundbreaking practices in corporate America was the President's Summit for America's Future, held in Philadelphia in April 1997. The conference featured President Clinton, former presidents Bush, Carter and Ford, Nancy Reagan, and General Colin Powell. But the stars were the numerous corporations providing support for the nation's youth in the areas of education, training, and health care.

Oracle Corporation, for example, committed $100 million to equip schools with network computers while the pharmacological company SmithKline Beecham committed $1.4 million to local Healthy Start initiatives as well as $1.5 million in "venture capital" to be matched by healthcare companies or philanthropic organizations.

Many of the commitments made at the summit were expansions of existing corporate social responsibility strategies. For instance, AT&T committed at least 100,000 hours of mentoring, tutoring, and coaching in forty communities through its AT&T Cares program, in addition to directing at least $30 million in grants and $60 million in product services by the year 2000 to provide schools with up-to-date information technology, among other pledges. The American Express Company committed more than $10 million through 2000 to help prepare young people for career success in the hospitality, food-service, lodging, retail, and other industries. And McDonald's/Ronald McDonald House Charities committed $100 million over the next five years to continue its work with children and families, including creating barrier-free playgrounds, providing educational opportunities for inner city youth, and dealing with issues like child abuse, youth suicide, and substance abuse.

In other words, much of the success of the Volunteer Summit was due to the fact that business had been already been doing programs like this for years. The summit was politics at its best. The press covered it, the pundits debated it, and the private and nonprofit sectors continued doing what they had been doing all along.

We're not making fun of the event. We just want to remind you what this book is really about: making money while making a difference. Don't let all the political, self-congratulatory fluff turn you off to the reality. Being a good and strategic corporate citizen pays off.

In 1995, when his company was honored by Hillary Clinton for being "family friendly," James Shiro, CEO of Price Waterhouse, said that pro-family projects "make good business sense... We realize the positive benefits these have on our bottom line."

Good community relations can also mean the difference between penetrating a new market or being ridden out of town on a rail. Wal-Mart was prevented from opening stores in Massachusetts and Vermont by activist groups worried about the retail chain's effect on their local economies. Monsanto was unable to open a new plant in Bowling Green, Kentucky. And even Walt Disney fell victim to strong community opposition to building a theme park on a Civil War battlefield in Northern Virginia, after spending millions on the planning process. The community felt that the Disney park would damage their quality of life.

When you build relationships that create trust within a community, the results are much more profitable:

> When the British firm GrandMetropolitan announced its plan to acquire Pillsbury, special interest groups and organizations from Minneapolis held a rally to publicize the disastrous impact on the community. The locals feared losing Pillsbury's charitable giving budget. GrandMetropolitan quickly responded with a pledge to maintain the Pillsbury heritage and thereby gained community support.

> During the 1992 Los Angeles riots, none of the thirty-one McDonald's restaurants in the area were looted or burned, although numerous other businesses were. McDonald's claims this is the "real payoff" for good community relations.

> One of the masters at this process is Merck. In a strategy Merck calls "site-based community relations," managers are expected to attend community meetings and build relationships with influential members of the community. When the company moved its headquarters from Rahway, New Jersey, to Whitehouse Station, it sent a community relations manager two years before the move. The manager interviewed neighbors of the proposed site—their requests led to design changes. Merck was praised in a *New York Times* article for being receptive to community needs.

> Merck's strategy even helped them survive a toxic chemical leak. On July 27, 1995, Merck's Flint River pharmaceutical plant in Albany, Georgia leaked a toxic cloud of phosphorous trichloride. 400 workers had to be evacuated, and forty-five people were hospitalized. Did

this mini-Bophal effect Merck's community relations? According to an article by Edmund Burke in the May/June 1997 issue of *Business Ethics*, the community's response to the leak was "nonchalant, sometimes laudatory." The director of a local daycare center said, "I've never had any reason to be concerned about Merck." And the compliance officer with the Georgia EDP hazardous waste unit described Merck as "environmentally conscious."

The challenge to corporations is to become a "neighbor of choice" and integrate community concerns into business planning decisions. Many companies are doing just that. Motorola, Polaroid, and Nova, for example, have their general managers attend executive education seminars in community relations.

Still Wondering "Why Now?"

In 1999's State of the Union Address, President Bill Clinton said, "Somehow we have to find a common ground on which business and workers, and environmentalists, and farmers, and government can stand together." He was echoing the sentiments of many Americans, that the line between business and the rest of the world is blurring.

Socially responsible investment funds are attracting record capital ($800 billion in 1994, up from $100 billion in 1985). According to the 1994 Walker study, 26 percent of potential investors said social responsibility was extremely important in making investment decisions. And 21 percent of current investors said they always check on values and ethics before investing. Consumers are spending more money to buy products that protect the environment.

We have seen the rise of the caring consumer who uses his or her wallet to demand that business change—consumers who believe that business must not only stop creating problems, it must also start creating solutions.

Can business afford to respond to these demands? Can it afford not to? Growth in the next millennium will come from strengthened relationships with consumers, and a company's reputation will become crucial to its success. Companies that invest in environmental controls, community development, work-force training, customer service, and responsible citizenship will buy consumer loyalty in years to come.

4

THE DANGERS OF STRATEGIC ALLIANCES

"You never hear the bullet that kills you."

— *Old Soldier's Proverb*

<   <   <   <

Some of you have been reading this book and wondering, "So what's the catch?" Make money, do good, there's got to be a deal with the Devil here someplace.

There is.

You have to be sincere. You have to be honest. You have to actually do good, not just do things that make it look like you're doing good.

The worst part is that even if you do it all right, even if you're pure of heart and ethical beyond measure, there are still going to be cynics out there who believe that partnerships between corporations and nonprofits have nothing to do with helping a worthy cause and everything to do with generating sales.

Don't be surprised. Remember, you used to say, "Never trust anyone over thirty." Since the mid 1980s, thousands of businesses have tied sales promotions to nonprofit causes. Everything from toasters to teddy bears has been sold "to benefit" a worthy cause. How could consumers not become a little cynical?

There's another reason for them to be cynical, too. The last two decades have seen too many examples of nonprofits that have violated the public trust, whether by the actions of individuals within them or through their own policies. When the reputation of an organization like the United Way can be immeasurably harmed by the actions of its president (who spent $600,000 of UW funds on his mistress), how can the public know who to trust?

Of course, the bright side is that many of those cynics have already sentenced you to eternal damnation for being in business in the first place. In other words, their cynicism is no reason to avoid creating good, powerful, effective, and sincere strategic alliances. Well-planned campaigns that truly benefit both partners receive praise rather than criticism.

So as you consider a strategic partnership, we'd like to make you aware of the criticisms some campaigns have received. Knowing the kind of heat you might draw in advance will help you design your own venture to be honest, mutually beneficial, and successful.

Using a Nonprofit

You hear it from every direction: consumers, consumer advocates, nonprofits, and even corporations. "Big businesses just use nonprofits for their own gains, to whitewash their images. It's baptism by blood-money." This is a serious accusation. In our society nonprofits are held in high esteem precisely because they are not commercial—because they exist for the public good and not for the benefit of individuals. We invest nonprofits with a high degree of purity, and using a nonprofit for commercial purposes violates that purity. Companies that do it risk harming their image. Nonprofits that allow it run the same risk.

And in some instances, the accusations may be well founded.

Witness the case of Philip Morris and the Bill of Rights. In 1989 the cigarette manufacturer announced it was spending $60 million to celebrate the 200th anniversary of the signing of the Bill of Rights. The celebration would include a traveling exhibition, which would take the document to all fifty states, and an ad campaign touting America's political freedoms. Assisting the company in this endeavor—for the sum of $600,000—was the National Archives, repository of the document and of other historical materials used in the campaign.

No sooner did the first ad (a view of the Capitol rotunda with voices of former presidents and other leaders reading from the Bill of Rights, followed by the Philip Morris logo) hit the airwaves than a hue and cry erupted from consumers and health organizations, decrying the campaign as a sleazy attempt to use a national symbol to reinforce the company's own campaign for smokers' rights. As the Bill of Rights toured the country, anti-smoking groups appeared on the evening news picketing the exhibition at almost every stop.

From a public relations standpoint, the campaign was a disaster. The National Archives didn't fare much better. It, too, was criticized, for having allowed itself to be "bought" for so commercial a venture.

Whether Philip Morris was sincere or not, whether allowing people around the country to see the actual the Bill of Rights was valuable or not, any benefit was lost in the torrent of criticism.

In fact, determining sincerity can be difficult. In 1996, U.S. Tobacco pledged a $1 million donation from sales of smokeless tobacco to the National Volunteer Fire Council. U.S. Tobacco makes Skoal and Copenhagen snuff, but tobacco in a different form is a leading cause of household fires. Was this a sincere effort, or an attempted whitewash?

In the past few years Exxon has been pumping money into the "Save the Tiger Fund," a five-year joint effort with the National Fish and Wildlife Fund. Critics are quick to point out that the tiger has long been the corporate logo for Exxon—do you remember, "Put a tiger in your tank?" Is this image building, oil-spill whitewash, or a sincere effort?

Starbuck's got involved in a cause-related marketing venture with CARE, who among their many projects provides clean water systems to villages in Guatemala. But they only got involved after it was revealed in 1994 that Starbuck's was buying beans from Guatemalan suppliers who paid their workers as little as $2.50 a day. Were they trying to make amends or trying to cover the stain of cheap coffee beans?

A campaign can draw scorn from consumers for using a nonprofit for other reasons, too. After the San Francisco earthquake in 1989, Burger King announced that each time someone ordered its new BK Double Burger it would give twenty-five cents to the Red Cross to aid earthquake victims. Even though the campaign raised $3 million in its first two weeks, Burger King was perceived by some as attempting to capitalize on a disaster to promote a new product.

Once again, the lesson is clear: even when you succeed in doing good, you may lose the public relations battle. Choose your causes wisely.

Buying a Nonprofit

A second criticism of strategic alliances is that participating nonprofits will lose their programmatic independence, becoming pawns of their corporate partners. This concern is understandable. At a time of declining government grants, nonprofits' need for money is at an all-time high. In their desire to attract corporate funds, the temptation is real to tailor what they do to corporate interests. Corporations, perceiving the marketing potential involved, are not shy about asking for favors.

We see this clearly in the case of museums. Where corporate donors used to be satisfied getting their names on a panel next to the exhibition title, today's exhibition sponsors are requesting—and sometimes getting—a lot more. The Formica Corporation, for instance, organized, curated, and helped underwrite several exhibits that visited museums around the country; the shows featured works made with the company's materials. Tiffany & Company initiated and paid for exhibits showcasing its jewelry and silver, which visited the Field Museum of Natural History in Chicago and the Museum of Fine Arts in Boston. Other companies have made similar arrangements. Should museums accept these company-initiated shows? Or do they reflect a bending of museum standards in order to attract sponsors and make money?

Environmental groups, too, have been accused of selling out to corporate interests. The World Wildlife Fund, the National Wildlife Federation, and the Audubon Society have all received large grants from corporations whose environmental records are poor. The agencies claim that they can remain objective regardless of who's paying the bills. Others say that its better to save a species with blood money than allow it to be lost forever on principle. But skeptics are not so sure. The corporate sugar daddies don't come out smelling like roses, either. Chevron, Mobil, Exxon, and other companies have been accused of buying off their adversaries by funding the groups that oppose their environmental practices.

Corporate interests can show up in the strangest places—including the chests of a hundred thousand Boy Scouts. Back in the early 1990s, the British Boy Scouts introduced a program in which a corporation could buy the right to place its name and logo on a merit badge for three years. The cost of the sponsorship varied with the badge's popularity. The athletic badge (bought by Pentland Industries) cost about £45,000 ($78,000). Other badges sold for between £5,000 and £50,000; Meccano, a French toy manufacturer, bought the craftsman badge, and the retail chain Asda bought the naturalist badge. Across the Atlantic The Boy Scouts of America have detailed guidelines concerning what type of commercial sponsorship is appropriate for their organization. Not appropriate, they say, is the use of uniformed Scouts to advertise a commercial product.

Even the 150-year-old American Medical Association (AMA) is not above the accusation of selling out, and in their case the results were disastrous. In August 1997 the AMA and Sunbeam entered into a five-year exclusive agreement that would allow Sunbeam to put the AMA's Seal of Approval on nine categories of home healthcare products. In exchange for the implied endorsement, Sunbeam would include AMA educational materials in the products and pay a royalty to the AMA on their sale.

When the public heard about the deal, there was an immediate outcry from the AMA membership, as well as consumer advocates and watchdog groups. They claimed that the endorsement would compromise the integrity of the AMA. This despite the AMA's intended use of the proceeds—which some estimates put at potentially millions of dollars—for research, education, and prevention programs on women's health, family violence, smoking and other important issues. The negative response grew so great that the AMA backed out of the arrangement. At the time of the deal, Sunbeam was being run by the infamous "Chainsaw" Al Dunlap, who promptly sued the AMA to live up to the contract. By the time the smoke cleared, three top AMA executives had lost their jobs, and the AMA's reputation and integrity were in critical condition.

Are the nonprofits being bought? Are the corporations buying—or merely helping? Nobody knows for sure, but even the suspicion can damage reputations.

The Loss of Traditional Philanthropy?

A third criticism leveled at strategic alliances is that it will jeopardize traditional, "pure" philanthropy. If corporations can get something in exchange for their dollars, will they continue to give money with no *quid pro quo*? Evidence suggests they will. Purely philanthropic corporate donations have actually risen since the late 1980s, when strategic alliances first began to gather steam.

If anything, the rise of strategic alliances has opened up more corporate money for nonprofits, since nonprofits can now tap corporate marketing as well as philanthropic budgets. According to an article in the May/June 1994 issue of the *Harvard Business Review* titled "The New Corporate Philanthropy," the size of the average grant from Fortune 500 companies has risen from less than $5,000 to more than $30,000. The Conference Board reported in 1995 that although 90 percent of companies have separate charitable giving budgets, 33 percent of companies also use public affairs budgets for some portion of their donations, and 27 percent of companies allocate money from their marketing budgets.

Corporations are discovering that this new "hybrid philanthropy" serves multiple corporate goals. When philanthropy managers and marketing managers get together, when human resources managers are invited into planning sessions with giving managers, interesting corporate synergies form. It might not be "traditional philanthropy," but can anyone say it's less effective?

A related concern is that strategic alliances will cause a decline in individual contributions. If people believe they've contributed to a cause by buying a product or attending an event, will they still write a check when a solicitation letter comes in the mail? Again, evidence suggests this is not a problem. Like corporate contributions, individual donations have steadily risen since the mid 1980s.

Of course, different sources have different takes on whether this is a real rise, an adjusted rise, a drop, a rise among itemized deductions, a drop among non-itemizers, a rise among the once rich who are now poor... well, you get the picture. Regardless, strategic partnerships offer a new way to funnel money into nonprofits. This shouldn't come as a surprise, since one of the biggest goals of strategic alliance campaigns is to draw attention to the needs of nonprofits and recruit new donors. Successful campaigns should increase donations, not siphon them away.

Will Only "Sexy" Nonprofits Benefit?

In the early days of strategic alliances a common criticism was that corporations would choose as their partners only "sexy" or "mediagenic" nonprofits. Critics within the nonprofit community feared that while these popular causes might benefit greatly from the strategy, the majority of agencies would be left out. Causes such as battered women, homeless people, and people with AIDS would be too depressing to make good strategic alliances.

In fact, some of the biggest and most-publicized strategic alliances in history have targeted precisely those "unsexy" groups. Hands Across America, for example, a 1986 made-for-TV mega event, cajoled hundreds of thousands of people into joining hands in a coast-to-coast human chain to raise money for the homeless. Corporations shelled out millions of dollars in cash and in-kind donations. Comic Relief returns year after year to tell jokes and raise money for the homeless. In a 1987 campaign, called Shelter Aid, Johnson & Johnson raised more than $1.5 million for battered women's shelters. The campaign was the company's most successful promotion ever. And the red ribbons of support for the victims of AIDS have become virtually ubiquitous among the socially aware.

Does this mean that the traditional causes were no longer sexy? Not according to the supporters of the American Cancer Society, the March of Dimes, or the American Red Cross.

It seems one of the truths about strategic alliances is that virtually any kind of issue will work because every cause and every nonprofit appeals to a particular audience. Johnson & Johnson chose battered women because the company believed that would appeal to its target market—women. Levi Strauss & Co. gives money to AIDS projects in part because the corporation knows that many of its young urban customers feel strongly about the issue. First Interstate Bank of California created a credit card for the Foundation for Wild Sheep in which a percentage of every purchase made with the card was given to the Foundation because even that esoteric organization had a membership base worth pursuing.

There are two lessons here. One is that every cause has a following, and for companies that want to attract that following, strategic alliances can be an effective vehicle. And two is that there's always somebody ready to criticize that which they fear or don't understand, even among the "good guys."

Fostering Nonprofit Dependence

Yet another concern sometimes voiced by critics of strategic alliances is that nonprofits will become dependent on their corporate partners for money and will suffer once a strategic alliance campaign ends.

For instance, think about the St. Clair County, Illinois Sheriff's Department. Their squad cars carry advertising for Barcom Electronics, a local alarm company. Barcom pays the county $6,000 a year to put their company name, phone number and a logo on the cars in addition to the usual Sheriff's Department markings. The county uses the money for a drug-awareness program. As it stands, it's hard to imagine a problem with this arrangement. The county gets a needed program, and Barcom gets "instant credibility," according to Barcom executive Mike Bartle. But what if the county relied on the funds for something more critical, such as vehicle maintenance, or even salaries? Could Barcom gain undue influence over the department? If Barcom pulled their sponsorship, might the Sheriff's Department be left hanging?

Like the previous criticism, this one doesn't carry a lot of weight. Nonprofits face a constant struggle for multiple and diverse sources of income. No nonprofit goes into any partnership with a corporation thinking it will last forever, or that he can ignore other donors. They know any source of funding supplements, rather than replaces, existing funds.

Nonetheless, companies that want to address this concern can help their nonprofit partners develop long-term strategies for increasing revenues. They can actively recruit donors among their employees and customers. They can lend their marketing staffs to help their partners develop fundraising campaigns. They can help their partners develop long-range plans that include new sources of income.

Cash is just one thing a corporation has to offer a nonprofit partner. Marketing and managerial support can be every bit as helpful in the long run. In fact, more than any cash donation, strategic alliances have the potential to make nonprofits independent and self-reliant.

Avoiding Criticism

So how can companies engaging in strategic alliances dodge the bullet? The answer is simple: be sincere. If your campaign is honorable in intent, it should be honorably perceived. If you genuinely support your partner—if your campaign does as much for the nonprofit as it does for you—the public should believe you.

Body Shop International is a retailer of natural, cruelty-free cosmetics, widely recognized for its socially responsible business practices. Posters and literature in Body Shop stores promote environmental causes. Sales people are given time off to volunteer. The company builds plants in depressed areas to stimulate local economies. Body Shop's 50 percent annual growth in the last decade is largely attributed to its social policies. Anita Roddick, Body Shop founder, has been a vocal advocate of corporations adopting social causes, and an equally strong critic of companies that do so insincerely. She warns: "[Consumers] can sniff out integrity and sniff out dishonesty, and know instinctively what is junk and what is true. They can spot arrogant jargon."

Usually, the campaigns that backfire are the ones that are designed strictly as sales promotions. See our ad! Buy our product! Help support our cause! The trouble is, in three short months the campaign is over and the cause is never mentioned again. How committed can that company be?

The campaigns that work are the ones in which the company truly supports the cause—and shows it time and time again. The company makes donations. It lends employees. It touts the cause in its ads. Sure, it invites the public to help by purchasing products or attending events. But it does an equal amount on its own. Those are partnerships you can believe in.

So if you want to establish a strategic alliance—and remain above reproach—be sincere. Pick a cause you believe in. Then find as many ways as possible to express that belief. Communicate your partner's message in your ads. Make in-kind donations. Encourage employees to volunteer. Create a long-term partnership in which you remind the public over and over of your commitment. If you believe in your partnership, the public will believe in it, too.

We're not saying it will be easy. We're not saying you won't draw unfair criticism. What we are saying is that it works.

You really can increase company profits and make the world a better place. All it takes is vision. And effort. And sincerity. And perseverance. And conviction. Like everything important, you have to work at it.

Changing the world is never easy. It takes sacrifice and commitment. People bleed to do it. People die to do it.

But today, you can change the world by doing your job—and if you do it with integrity and ability, you can achieve amazing results.

PART II

STRATEGIC ALLIANCE OPTIONS

5

CAUSE-RELATED MARKETING

"[Cause-related marketing has the] ability to enhance corporate image, to differentiate products, and to increase sales and loyalty. Cause-related marketing is enlightened self-interest, a win-win business situation."

—Dominic Cadbury
Chairman
Cadbury Schweppes

<   <   <   <

It's time to look more closely at the different forms strategic alliances can take, and some of the most successful examples of each. And we want to warn you: the lines of demarcation can get murky. Where does cause-related marketing end and licensing begin? Aren't some strategic philanthropic donations just charitable versions of sponsorships?

We'll let you in on a little secret: much of the difference is semantic, although some is merely legal. Just like some people get upset with strategic philanthropy, and claim it really isn't philanthropy at all, there are "experts" who are willing to go to verbal war over the use of the term "cause-related marketing."

So what is CRM? Business in the Community, a UK charity sponsored by leading businesses and social forces, in their 1998 publication, "The Cause-Related Marketing Guidelines," offers this definition:

> Cause-Related Marketing (CRM) is a commercial activity by which businesses and charities or causes form a partnership with each other to market an image, product or service for mutual benefit. It is an additional tool for addressing the social issues of the day through providing resources and funding whilst at the same time addressing business marketing objectives.

In "traditional" CRM, a corporation and a nonprofit enter a joint promotional campaign. Packaging, advertising, and other forms of communication encourage consumers to purchase the corporation's products, knowing that a percentage of each sale will go to the nonprofit. Most often this is done through the use of cents-off coupons: for each coupon redeemed, the corporation donates a fixed amount to the nonprofit, frequently up to a predetermined ceiling. By cashing in on consumer interest in a worthy cause, corporations are generally able to increase sales while generating goodwill. Nonprofits benefit by raising money, and by having their name and message widely broadcast.

Cause-related marketing is just that: marketing. A commercial activity. It has a philanthropic result, but its primary purpose is sales. It requires a consumer to buy a company's product or service in order to benefit the cause.

Terms have a tendency to change with time and usage. Practices that were not strictly "traditional" CRM, such as event sponsorship or strategic philanthropy, are now commonly referred to under the cause-related marketing umbrella.

Before we move on to describe the various options you have when engaging in cause-related marketing, we'll leave you with a suggestion. If it's honest and sincere, and it works, and it makes the world a better place and your company more profitable, don't get too hung up on what to call it.

Cause-Related Marketing

Most people believe there must be a secret formula to cause-related marketing. How can you lower prices, give money to a cause, and still increase profits? There must be a trick.

We admit it. There is.

The secret is that when you make a lower profit margin, and give the difference to a worthy cause, and consumers know it, they buy more. Sales go up. And, as we all know, increased sales can not only offset lower profit margins, they can send profits through the roof.

Pillsbury knows it, too. In the first full year of their Customer Community Partnerships CRM effort, they engaged in twenty customer partnerships in thirty-nine communities around the United States. They benefited forty-seven youth-serving nonprofits including Big Brothers/Big Sisters of America, Boys

& Girls Clubs of America, and Second Harvest Kids' Cafe. The result? Sales volume increases ranging between 20 percent and 185 percent. And that doesn't even take into account the publicity Pillsbury gained at their check presentation events, which were covered in the media. Or their strengthened relationships with retailers.

Who says there's no such thing as a win-win-win proposition in business? Corporations that engage in CRM earn money and goodwill. Nonprofits gain money and exposure. But consumers drive the success of CRM. Surveys show they are willing to change, but they don't say why. We think it's a pretty simple reason.

Empowerment.

Think of yourself. When you go to the store, you're pretty much stuck with your choices. This cereal tastes better, that one's cheaper. This toilet paper's recycled, that one's soft. Sure, you have a choice, but no power. Enter CRM. When you buy a CRM product, your choice has an impact on something other than your stomach or your backside. You can save the rainforest, or fight illiteracy, or help cure a disease. You're still buying a product, which you were going to do anyway. But now, you're also helping to change the world.

Cause-related marketing turns capitalism into a philanthropic tool.

CRM needs little introduction. Only a Rip Van Winkle could have missed the flurry of cents-off coupons tied to charities that showed up on everything from cereal to toilet tissue during the late 1980s. In fact, the strategy became so ubiquitous that, by the early 1990s, many large marketers believed it had lost its appeal and eliminated or reduced their CRM campaigns.

Reports of the death of CRM were greatly exaggerated, and today CRM has made a comeback.

In the 1996 Roper Starch survey, executives from seventy firms across the United States were interviewed and 93 percent reported that they engage in cause-related marketing to build deeper relationships with their customers. They see it as a powerful tool for building brand loyalty and lifelong customer bonds. Among other reasons for engaging in CRM, executives reported enhancing corporate image and reputation, creating new platforms, creating or maintaining a compelling corporate purpose, and differentiating a product or service. Nine out of ten executives were pleased with the results of their initiatives.

In the United Kingdom, executives are recognizing the growing importance of CRM. A 1996 CRM Corporate Survey Report of 450 United Kingdom companies by Business in the Community found that 70 percent of marketing directors, 67 percent of community affairs directors and 59 percent of CEOs all believe CRM will increase in importance over the next two-to-three years. The survey also found that 56 percent of CEOs view CRM as being important to the overall aims of their company. And 56 percent of marketing directors and 68 percent of community affairs directors state that CRM held obvious benefits for both sides.

Everybody's practicing CRM—big companies, small companies, and even companies that defy traditional terminology, like Newman's Own Inc. (More on him later.)

CRM has proven itself to be a gold mine for generating sales for companies and revenue for nonprofits. Its value is unassailable. The question now is not whether or not to do CRM, but how to do it well.

How It All Began

CRM burst onto the national scene in 1983 when American Express joined the project to restore the Statue of Liberty and Ellis Island. AmEx spent $6 million in a highly visible advertising campaign, making sure everybody knew what they were doing. Specifically, America Express promised that during a three-month period, they would make the following donations to the Statue of Liberty/Ellis Island Restoration Fund:

> A percentage of each purchase made with an American Express card;
> A percentage of each AmEx "travel package" over $500;
> A percentage of sales of American Express Travelers' Cheques;
> A percentage of each new card application.

The results of the campaign made marketing history. AmEx card use rose 28 percent, new card applications rose 17 percent, and the campaign raised $1.7 million for the Statue of Liberty and Ellis Island.

American Express even gained a benefit they didn't pay for: the campaign was so successful that most people thought they were an official sponsor of the restoration, although the company had never actually paid to be one.

American Express had actually been practicing CRM since 1981, when it developed the concept in response to three clearly defined marketing goals:

1. To convince consumers to acquire and use AmEx charge cards;
2. To convince more businesses to accept the cards;
3. To find newsworthy ways of doing it.

The company was also aware of a growing demand for corporations to be socially responsible—to give back to the communities in which they did business. Could "giving back to the community" somehow be linked to card purchases and card use? Was it a newsworthy marketing tool? As managers pondered the possibilities, they realized they had more to offer a community than money. Their ability to create powerful promotional campaigns could be extremely beneficial to nonprofit organizations with small budgets but big messages to get out.

From this examination of multiple needs came the strategy. In selected markets—communities where the company wanted to expand—American Express tied its business to an arts group (an orchestra, a theater, a museum), something it knew would interest card holders. Large advertising campaigns urged consumers to shop, dine, and travel using the American Express card, because every purchase would benefit the selected organization. The ads also touted the strengths of the arts groups, providing significant exposure for their causes.

The man most commonly credited with American Express's strategy is Jerry Welsh, then executive VP of worldwide marketing. The first local promotion was to support the arts in San Francisco. Every time someone in the San Francisco area used their American Express card, the corporation donated five cents to a variety of local arts programs. Every new card member that signed up netted the arts a whopping two dollars. All told, local arts programs received $108,000.

These and other local campaigns worked. In every one, card use rose and local media picked up the story, generating the publicity the company wanted. The arts groups received unrestricted income, as well as tremendous public exposure. Some groups received benefits beyond those anticipated as their donations, memberships, and business connections increased.

The success of the Statue of Liberty campaign encouraged American Express to spend $23.5 million to advertise sixty-seven other charitable promotions, which generated over $9.3 million in contributions to nonprofits around the world.

In 1983 American Express made the Statue of Liberty the first national CRM campaign, which spawned thousands of similar CRM ventures between consumer-oriented corporations and nonprofits. Partners have included large national organizations like the Red Cross and MasterCard, as well as small-town social service agencies working with local retailers.

In some instances, cause-related marketing is driven by the needs of a non-profit cause. The March of Dimes Birth Defects Foundation wanted to raise awareness of the need for folic acid in pregnant women. Folic Acid is a B vitamin, which studies show can help prevent certain birth defects, most commonly in the brain and spine. Kellogg's Product 19 cereal was rich in Folic Acid. So the March of Dimes and Kellogg entered into a CRM venture where both benefited. Kellogg got to put the March of Dimes name on boxes of Product 19, and the March of Dimes got to disseminate their message about the benefits of folic acid, along with a donation of $100,000 from Kellogg.

More often, though, corporations have sought out nonprofits. Some of the larger, nationally known nonprofits have received so many requests for partnerships that they have created full-time staff positions to develop and manage CRM programs. The added staff expense is well worth it, since Big Brothers/Big Sisters, the Special Olympics, the American Cancer Society, and the American Heart Association have all raised millions of dollars through CRM campaigns. Smaller nonprofits have raised smaller amounts—generally less than 10 percent of their annual income—but the secondary benefits of exposure, public education, and recruitment of members, volunteers, and new donors add to the campaigns' value.

On the profit side, corporations obviously love the results of CRM. The Texize Division of Dow Consumer Products Company, manufacturer of household cleaners, announced its best quarter ever after a CRM campaign with the National Crime Prevention Council. Scott Paper Company's CRM campaign for Ronald McDonald Houses was the most successful sales promotion in Scott history. Johnson & Johnson has described its CRM campaign, Shelter Aid, as its most successful promotion ever (see their story below). And

Fred Wilkinson, senior vice president for corporate initiatives at American Express, says the company's cause-related marketing programs have produced results "at least as good as, and frequently better than" conventional marketing programs.

Thousands of smaller companies have also found CRM campaigns extremely effective at generating sales and consumer interest. CRM has helped companies strengthen their image as good community citizens. It even has a residual effect on employees, sales forces, and franchisees, who have responded with interest, pride, and improved morale to CRM efforts.

One of the benefits of CRM is that you can use it for just about anything. For a fairly simple strategy, it's remarkably flexible. It can be tailored to a company's specific marketing needs. Let's look at some of the ways other companies have applied CRM to reach their objectives.

Boosting Sales of a Single Brand
Procter & Gamble (Italy) and ActionAID (Ethiopia)

Many companies use CRM to boost the sales of a single brand. By linking the brand with a nonprofit, corporations can reinforce the brand's existing image, or even create an entirely new one. They can gain the attention of a particular audience, encouraging new consumers to give the brand a try.

In Italy, Dash soap powder already owned 27 percent of the soap powder market. But there's always room for growth, so Procter & Gamble launched a CRM campaign with ActionAID to build schools, health clinics, and hospitals in Ethiopia. By the time the campaign was over, 170,000 consumers had contributed to the effort. P&G matched their contributions, yielding ten times the expected income for ActionAID and providing 14,000 people with new access to health care. And sales of Dash rose by five percent in the Italian market.

Pumping an Entire Product Line
Johnson & Johnson and the American Red Cross

Rather than focusing on a single brand, some companies use CRM to promote an entire product line. The benefits of this strategy: increased marketing efficiency, increased sales of several products with a single campaign, and building brand image across the entire line. The caveat: all the products must logically relate to the cause and the nonprofit.

Johnson & Johnson wanted to reinforce the quality and breadth of its line of first-aid products. Who is the first name in first aid? The American Red Cross. So Johnson & Johnson created an across-the-line CRM venture: each time a consumer redeemed a coupon for Band-Aids, gauze pads, or other first-aid items, the company gave a percentage of the sale to the Red Cross. The obvious connection between the product line and the nonprofit made the campaign work.

Cross-Promoting Products from Different Companies

The International Red Cross and HelpAd

In anticipation of an operating shortfall, the International Red Cross (IRC) came up with a CRM concept that only they could pull off. With their program, HelpAd, companies are given the opportunity to cross-promote their products on the packages of complimentary products. For instance, Green Giant will cross promote their canned sweet corn with Dolmio sauces to encourage consumers to combine their products with other ingredients. Participating brands can feature the HelpAd/Red Cross logo on their packages. The first companies to sign up included Pizza Hut, The Body Shop, SmithKline Beecham, Tesco, GrandMetropolitan, and Van den Bergh Foods. The promotion will kick off with a £1 million ad campaign. The IRC is hoping to grab a one percent share of the $250 billion spent worldwide annually on advertising. According to Paul Adams, director of HelpAd, "We could have launched an aggressive global fundraising campaign to boost donations, but this would have been only a short-term solution. Our aim is to improve the lot of those in need over the longer term. We don't want to divert money from other organizations, we want to find money in new ways." Would you expect anything less from an organization that could bring candy and humane treatment to prison camps in time of war?

Reinforcing a Company's Image

Johnson & Johnson and Shelter Aid

Some companies have used CRM to boost or reinforce their corporate image by tying virtually all their brands to a cause. This can be tricky to pull off, since it requires a cause and a nonprofit that relate strongly to all the brands. Johnson & Johnson was able to do it because the company makes a wide variety of products, but all are marketed to the same consumers: women. In 1987 Johnson & Johnson created a nine-brand CRM campaign around the cause of battered women that was, according to J&J, the most successful promotion in their history. The Shelter Aid campaign raised $1.5 million to establish and staff the first year of a toll-free hotline for abused women and donated money to a nationwide network of battered women's shelters. Four Johnson & Johnson business units joined in the campaign, which featured products ranging from baby shampoo to tampons. The campaign resulted in significant market share increases for participating brands, and the StayFree line of feminine hygiene products experienced a dramatic increase in sales.

Changing a Company's Image
Norwich Union Insurance and St. John Ambulance

Johnson & Johnson used CRM to reinforce their image to their target audience. In the UK, Norwich Union insurance used CRM to change their image entirely.

Norwich Union is one of the largest insurance firms in the UK, with £49 billion of funds under management and operations around the world. It was known as a stuffy, boring company, an image it wanted to change. In September 1996, Norwich Union instituted its "First Aid in the Home" campaign. Television ads announced that Norwich was offering free first aid course training for 25,000 people. St. John Ambulance taught the courses, while Norwich picked up the tab. By the end of 1997, 13,000 people had been trained. St. John estimates that for every person trained, 50 are safer. So in addition to shining up its image and picking up 25,000 new customers, Norwich also helped protect over 650,000 people in the last few years.

Increase Retail Activity
Tesco vs. Sainsbury: The Schools Are the Winners

With retailers often carrying the same selection of products, price wars between competing retailers are nothing new. But CRM wars? In the United Kingdom, Tesco's Computers for Schools program was so successful that Tesco's main competitor, Sainsbury, came up with a similar program of their own.

Tesco is the United Kingdom's number one food retailer, a huge chain with over 500 stores in the United Kingdom expanding into Europe at a rapid rate. Their fiercest rival is Sainsbury's supermarket chain. In 1992 Tesco introduced their Computers for Schools campaign. For every minimum purchase at Tesco (currently £10), shoppers received a voucher to give to their children's schools. Schools collect and redeem the vouchers for computers, software and other equipment. By the end of 1997, £34 million in equipment had been donated to over 11,000 schools, including 29,000 computers.

Competitor Sainsbury was not to be outdone. They first introduced their School Bags initiative, which offered vouchers for school supplies and equipment if shoppers reused their plastic shopping bags. 18,000 schools benefited from this program. In 1997, they launched the School Rewards program, which was similar to Tesco's in that shoppers who made a £10 purchase received a voucher for school equipment—although in addition to computers, schools could also purchase gym equipment and other needed items. According to their Web site, in 1997 Sainsbury's School Rewards program gave out more equipment than any other retailer in the United Kingdom. For 1998, they have done away with vouchers, linking the School Rewards directly to their electronic Shoppers' Rewards Cards.

Although the competition between Tesco and Sainsbury remains fierce, the fact that both retailers are expanding their programs means that not only are they both reaping benefits from their campaigns, but also that the real winners, the schools, will go on benefiting.

Strengthening Relationships with Retailers and Distributors
Pillsbury, Winn-Dixie, Publix, and Customer Community Partnerships

Competition for shelf space has become one of the most hotly contested areas of retailing in recent years. Earlier, we discussed Pillsbury's Customer Community Partnerships in terms of increased sales. But there was a side effect: stronger relationships with their retailers.

One of the retailers who joined Pillsbury's Customer Community Partnership program was Winn-Dixie of New Orleans. In August, 1995, they began a four-to-five-week promotion that included advertising and display of six Pillsbury product groups. Out of the optional charities Pillsbury had picked, Winn-Dixie chose the local Boys & Girls Clubs. Not only did Winn-

Dixie succeed in reinforcing their image as a concerned member of their community, but they also sold more product. Over the same period the previous year, sales of canned vegetables increased 36 percent, refrigerated baked goods rose 21 percent, and dry groceries were up nine percent.

Another retailer who signed up was Publix of Lakeland, Florida. They supported three nonprofits: the Thomasville YMCA, Boys & Girls Clubs of Bay County, and the Frank Callen Boys & Girls Club, Savannah. In a five-week promotion during August and September of 1995, they featured two or three items per category each week. They also added a corporate sale and a Bake-Off contest using Pillsbury products. The results: a total case sales increase of over 189 percent, as well as extensive media coverage.

In each case, the retailers received increased media coverage and experienced huge sales lifts thanks to joining Pillsbury's Customer Community Partnerships. Now which manufacturer do you think was more likely to get increased shelf space in the future?

How Long Should a CRM Campaign Last?

Pick the right answer:

> As long as possible for maximum opportunity for consumer response.
> As short a time as possible so it doesn't lose its appeal.

Actually, the real answer lies somewhere in between. Companies that engage in cause-related marketing walk a fine line between maximum exposure and consumer fatigue. And don't forget that a short campaign can be perceived as a lack of commitment to the cause itself. To find a safe middle ground, successful campaigns tend to follow one of the following patterns:

One-Week Campaigns > One week is a short period within which to advertise a campaign and get consumers to act. But it's been known to work—and work well—when tied to a specific event. Ralston Purina, for example, has timed a CRM campaign with the National Humane Society to coincide with National Pet Week. Tying a campaign to a preexisting event is a good way to generate additional publicity.

Three-Week Campaigns > Many successful campaigns last only three weeks. These are frequently timed for the period between Thanksgiving and Christmas, when shoppers are being reminded to "remember the needy." Food manufacturers and retailers often carry out their campaigns at this time, with the contributions going to food banks and homeless shelters.

Three-Month Campaigns > The majority of cents-off coupon campaigns last three months. That's long enough to generate sufficient publicity, establish a strong presence in consumers' minds, and give them time to buy. It's short enough that the campaign doesn't lose its novelty. It corresponds with a calendar quarter, making it easy to track results. And provable results make it easier to justify CRM campaigns.

Annual Campaigns > While most companies design CRM campaigns as single events, some build their campaigns into annual promotions. They occur each year at the same time, frequently in coordination with a preexisting event. Thus each year's campaign reinforces previous campaigns in consumers' minds. For example, Procter & Gamble carries out a CRM campaign with the Special Olympics every year, raising millions of dollars for the cause. The repetition of the campaign cements the association between the company and the Special Olympics, producing residual benefit to the company even at other times of the year.

Timing Is Everything—Or Is It?
New Covent Garden Soup Company and Crisis

Of course, there are also companies who don't believe in adhering to any guidelines at all.

Back when the New Covent Garden Soup Company started in 1988, it began a relationship with Crisis, the national charity for single homeless people in the UK. Originally, they simply wanted someone that would make good use of its surplus product. Crisis was a perfect match: it runs Crisis Open Houses, a network of homeless shelters sometimes referred to as "soup kitchens."

As part of their marketing, New Covent Garden runs CRM campaigns from time to time. In November 1996 they began a CRM program with a special flavor soup, Pea and Ham, on sale for only four months. Packaging carried information about Crisis, along with the phone number of the donations hotline. In addition, New Covent Garden promised to make a fixed donation to help install and refurbish kitchens in Crisis Open Houses.

New Covent picks unique periods for their CRM efforts. Earlier in 1996, they produced a special edition National Trust Wild Mushroom Soup for a five-month period, from January to May. Ten pence from every sale went to restore the garden at Fenton House, which grows, you guessed it, mushrooms.

The Danger in Cause-Related Marketing

The danger in cause-related marketing is that it looks so easy. So easy to make money. So easy to get in and out fast. So easy to be a hero. The trouble with that attitude is that it makes it so easy to fail. So easy for a campaign to backfire because it's perceived not as helping a nonprofit, but as using a nonprofit to sell a product. As more companies jump onto the CRM bandwagon, consumers are getting wiser. They can sniff out frauds and then expose them to the media and on the Internet. Even if they're wrong, they can undo any results you attain.

As we said before, you must be sincere. If you decide to pursue cause-related marketing, don't do it as a one-shot thing. Even if you choose one of the shorter-length CRM campaigns, make it part of a continuing partnership with a nonprofit that makes sense for your company to be involved with. Use other elements to enhance your campaign: in-kind donations, employee volunteers, special events. Extras like these will further the cause and let the world know you're really committed. Consumers will support your campaign because they support your partner. They want to know you genuinely support your partner, too.

The success stories we've related succeeded because they were sincere. Above all, remember the Philip Morris example from chapter 4. Consumers do.

6

SPONSORSHIP

"Condoms... what to wear when you're not wearing jeans."
—*Levi Strauss UK*
TV commercial for the Health Education Board of Scotland

<   <   <   <

Corporations have a long history of sponsoring symphony concerts, public television, art exhibitions, and special events with nonprofits. The International Events Group, a trade association, estimated that North American sponsorship spending alone reached $5.9 billion by the end of 1997. Thousands of companies sponsor sports races, art exhibits, symphony and rock concerts, walk-a-thons, bike-a-thons, and other events, mostly in partnership with nonprofit organizations. They run the gamut from low-budget local tie-ins to multi-million-dollar extravaganzas broadcast over national TV. Perhaps more than any other form of strategic alliance, event sponsorship holds something for everyone.

Take the case of the Tanqueray Gin AIDS Rides. The first ride, from San Francisco to Los Angeles in May 1994, changed forever the face of fundraising events for AIDS charities. The seven-day event raised approximately $1.6 million and spawned a series of rides across the country. By the end of 1997, there had been a dozen rides and total proceeds topped $40 million. In 1998 rides were scheduled for San Francisco to Los Angeles, Boston to New York, Minneapolis/St. Paul to Chicago, and in Washington, D.C., and Texas. Many people would be surprised to know that the first ride was designed not as "a charitable activity, but as a successful brand publicity event" by Tanqueray's brand development team.

Sponsorships are particularly well suited to a variety of corporate goals:

> Marketing goals can be met by designing an event to appeal to a target market. Retailers can be brought in to stimulate sales and traffic at the retail level. Merchandising opportunities can be built in to sell event-related products, which provide lasting in-home reminders.

> Community affairs goals can be met by designing an event that responds to needs in the community and includes the community in its implementation.

> Employee relations needs can be met by building in employee participation. Events can build pride and provide perks for employees.

> Philanthropic goals can be met by picking an event that falls within your corporate giving policy.

> Public relations goals can be met by designing an event that is unusual and therefore of interest to the media.

On the nonprofit side, the benefits are equally substantial. Events offer nonprofits a great way to get their message out—through the event itself and through attendant publicity. They spur people to action on the nonprofit's behalf—by collecting pledges, by attending a concert, by cleaning up a lake. And they can collect money from the public for the organization—through donations or an admission fee.

Events can be remarkably flexible, tailored to the needs of the partners. They can be big one-time national celebrations. They can be continuing national or international events that travel from city to city, being altered to fit each city along the way. Or they can be strictly local events that touch one city, or even one neighborhood. Special events can be tailored to an issue, to a geographic or socioeconomic market, and to a budget level.

They can even be made to give candy to a baby.

> At least, that's what Cadbury does every year in the United Kingdom. Every summer thousands of people take a ten-mile stroll around London in the Cadbury Strollerthon. The annual event raises £400,000 for Save the Children and One Small Step. Along the way, walkers sample over 85,000 Cadbury items, as well as providing their names for Cadbury's database.

Event sponsorship can be an important component of an ongoing strategic partnership, raising the program to new heights, as American Express discovered when they sponsored Taste of the Nation:

> Taste of the Nation is the largest annual food- and wine-tasting event in the United States. All the proceeds go to Share our Strength, the hunger relief organization with which American Express has had an ongoing relationships since 1988. It's hard to accuse American Express of using Share our Strength for their own purposes, especially when they've donated over $20 million to hunger prevention and relief since 1993.

Of course, event sponsorship has its downside, too. Some events can be logistical nightmares. They may require large numbers of bodies—paid or volunteer. They tend to have many details, which means lots of room for things to go wrong. They frequently depend on wholly undependable phenomena, like weather, or celebrities. And they require more of your time for organizing and orchestrating than some other forms of strategic partnerships. But if you have staff time and energy and a good nonprofit partner on whom you can depend for a lot of legwork, they can be well worth the hassles. And they provide something no other form of strategic alliance can—the event itself.

When we think of event sponsorship, it's easy to focus on the extravaganzas. Events can also be smaller affairs, designed to further corporate policy and generate new business among a select target audience:

> In an effort to explore the potential for new alliances between nonprofits and business, Chase invited the leaders of 400 major nonprofits to New York City for the Chase Not-for-Profit Forum. The

1994 program was the brainchild of Marlene Hess, vice president and director of not-for-profit relations at Chase. The major issue was how nonprofits can serve their communities and maintain quality of service during an era of budget tightening and increased competition for funding.

Events such as Chase's serve a variety of functions—new business development not the least among them. According to Hess, "We're determined to be the employer and provider of choice to the not-for-profit community." By bringing the nonprofit community together, Chase signals to the community that they are aware of and serious about the concerns facing nonprofits. It gives Chase the chance to show other nonprofits how it has already helped its current partners, whether in financial services, grants, sponsorships or public awareness. And since many of these partners were New York-based (New York Public Library, Police Athletic League, New York Cares Coat Drive, and the Child Vaccination program in league with NYNEX, Con Ed, the MTA, Children's Defense Fund, New York City Department of Health, and others), the forum gives Chase a sort of home-field advantage.

Even though event sponsorship has become the sexiest form of sponsorship, there are other forms of sponsorship. Another popular, albeit more traditional, form of sponsorship is when a corporation is the founding sponsor of a national youth service organization:

> City Year is a national service program that brings together young people from diverse backgrounds for a year of full-time community service. Launched exclusively with private funding, City Year is supported by a unique private-public partnership between foundations, corporations, individuals, state and local municipalities, and the AmeriCorps National Service Network. Since the program began, City Year has received over $21 million in cash donations. And that's not even taking into account any additional support, including computers, fax machines, headquarters space, consulting support, legal and audit services, volunteerism, uniforms, and boots.

Timberland was one of the founding sponsors of City Year, along with Digital and others. Their financial involvement has grown from a $50,000 Team Sponsorship in 1991 to an unprecedented $5 million investment in 1995 to their $1 million dollar challenge grant, which they made in 1997 in conjunction with America's Promise. They are the Official "Uniform Outfitter" of the City Year Corps, providing the Corps' signature red jackets.

The relationship between Timberland and City Year goes far beyond money and uniforms. Timberland CEO Jeffrey Swartz joined City Year's board of directors in 1992. The company has lent executives to work with City Year in corporate marketing, a commitment worth $5 million. Timberland hires City Year graduates to work in operations. And the partnership has even had an impact on Timberland's own community service program. Says CEO Swartz, "Many companies pay thousands upon thousands of dollars for the types of team-building skills we learn through giving of ourselves, together. So not only is Timberland furthering positive change and community betterment, we are making an investment in our infrastructure. This is not philanthropy. I firmly believe that the minds we turn on here at Timberland explode our productivity and effectiveness."

As the case of Timberland and City Year proves, events aren't the only form of sponsorship that can bring energy and excitement to your company. Which brings us to the new kid in town: sponsored advertising.

Sponsored Advertising

Sponsored advertising is a program in which a corporation buys advertising for a nonprofit and includes its own message in the ad. Compared to event sponsorship or ongoing support of an organization, sponsored advertising is simpler, less expensive, and equally effective.

Until sponsored advertising, nonprofits relied on public service announcements (PSAs) to get their messages out. These free ads are useful: they provide $3 billion of donated air time for nonprofits each year. They have their limitations, though. They tend to run at odd hours, wherever the stations can fit them in without sacrificing costly time slots, and rarely if ever in prime time. There is no way to target them to specific audiences. They are harder and harder to get as more nonprofits compete for the limited slots. And they are extremely expensive to produce, averaging $150,000—well beyond the budget of all but the largest nonprofits.

With sponsored advertising, the nonprofit often pays nothing for the production of the ad, which is usually more ambitious than the nonprofit could have contemplated. The ads are usually better targeted and run in better time slots. As a result, many nonprofit groups have eagerly embraced the concept of sponsored ads.

Corporations, too, have warmed to the concept. Sponsored ads provide all the benefits of any other form of nonprofit partnership. They establish or reinforce a company's connection with a worthy cause. They can enhance a product's credibility. They can distinguish a product from its competition and expose a company to new markets. They can even give a company an excuse for advertising at times when there are no "real" reasons (such as new product launches and holiday sales).

It's no wonder the number of sponsored ad campaigns is rising. In some cases, nonprofits are approaching corporations with ideas for ads that the two organizations then produce together. In others, charities have sold corporations ads that are already produced, to which the corporation adds its own brief message. Other campaigns have been initiated by corporations, which add a brief nonprofit message to their own product or image pitch.

Sponsored advertising is also an excellent way to expand your commitment to a cause, which is exactly what Levi Strauss & Co. has done on a worldwide scale:

> Ever since 1982, Levi Strauss & Company has been involved with AIDS issues. Headquartered in San Francisco, employee groups began volunteering to work with AIDS groups the year after the famous *New York Times* article brought AIDS to public awareness. Formal education of employees began in 1983, and since then, the company has made AIDS a major initiative both in the United States and abroad. By 1996, strategic philanthropic investment had reached

$14 million globally. This global commitment makes sense, since Levi Strauss & Co. is the world's largest brand-name apparel manufacturer, with over 35,000 employees worldwide.

In addition to strategic philanthropy, community involvement and workplace education, Levi Strauss & Co. has bolstered their efforts with some unique examples of sponsored advertisements.

In Great Britain they've partnered with the Health Education Board of Scotland (HEBS) to adapt television commercials to educate teens about safe sex. When HEBS approached the Levi Strauss UK marketing staff, they responded with a new campaign with a tag line that said "Condoms... what to wear when you're not wearing jeans." The commercials were shown in theaters around the country.

In India and Singapore Levi Strauss India and a local AIDS organization developed a prevention video shown in Levi's Only Stores.

Compared to other forms of sponsorship, sponsored advertising is still defining itself. There's plenty of room for innovation, as Northwest Airlines' Air Cares program shows. Northwest Airlines has invented a new form of strategic partnership that is one part sponsored advertising, one part in-kind donation, and one part entertainment:

> Every quarter Northwest Airlines has a captive—and restless—audience of ten million passengers that need entertaining. In 1994 they launched the Air Cares program, a strategic partnership between national and international nonprofits including Big Brothers/Big Sisters of America, the Pediatric AIDS Foundation and Kids for Saving Earth. The program spotlights one organization each quarter, with an in-flight video or announcement on every flight and an article in the airline's magazine, World Traveler. The article usually encourages travelers to donate to the cause via a postage paid envelope. In addition, Northwest has set up a program for frequent flyers to donate their World Perks mileage as a Fly-Write ticket to the nonprofit. Contributors of miles or $50 or more receive a 500-mile bonus

award from the airline. Northwest employees are also encouraged to volunteer for the partner nonprofits.

The nonprofit gets to deliver its fundraising, public awareness, and volunteer recruitment message to ten million passengers every three months. Northwest generates good public relations. And passengers are a little less bored, having had the opportunity to learn about a good cause, and maybe even to contribute to it.

The Negatives About Sponsored Advertising

You knew there had to be some, didn't you? Two concerns lead detractors of sponsored ads to see the strategy as dangerous rather than beneficial.

> The first is the concern that by linking their message with a corporate pitch, nonprofits are implicitly endorsing products. And while that is a danger, if you and your nonprofit partner work together you can craft sponsored advertising that never crosses the ethical line between helping the nonprofit and buying it.

> The second is the fear that the rise of sponsored ads will reduce the availability of public service announcements. If the media can get paid to run nonprofit ads, will they continue to run PSAs for free? So far there is no indication that they won't. Major media outlets have not reduced the number of PSA slots available, and most media experts believe that the two advertising techniques can coexist—as long as nonprofits don't ask for both free and paid space at the same time. Also, in many markets PSAs are a requirement for FCC licensing, which means they'll be around for a long, long time regardless of the popularity of sponsored ads.

In any event, sponsored ads are here to stay. Corporations like their effectiveness. Most nonprofits like their reach. As long as consumers place a high value on helping social causes, sponsored ads are likely to remain a strong weapon in a company's marketing arsenal.

7

PREMIUMS

"Mommy, buy me that one!"
— *Overheard in the supermarket*

<   <   <   <

When was the last time you walked down the cereal aisle in the supermarket? Do you remember how many cereals included premiums? Mini-comic books, NASCAR champ decals, Nickelodeon Slime, lunch boxes, trading cards, games, and so on?

Too many to count, right?

Premiums are huge, and for the most part they fall into three categories:

1. Premiums having to do with the product.
2. Premiums having to do with licensed properties.
3. Premiums having to do with nonprofits.

There's nothing new about the first two. Companies have been offering them for years. From secret decoder rings to movie tie-ins, premiums are everywhere. When you leave the hallowed aisles of the American supermarket for the trenches of corporate America, premiums get even more common. Think about the premiums at fast food restaurants alone!

Thankfully, the development of partnerships between corporations and nonprofits has put a whole new spin on the premium market. Finally, there's an alternative to giving customers that same old logo-bearing coffee mug. Or calendar. Or appointment book. Or decoder ring.

These days you can give them a customized product that truly reflects your business, that genuinely meets their need, and that comes with the credibility of a well-respected nonprofit. Is your market families? How about giving them a four-color book of games for the whole family, produced by a recognized expert in family education, the local children's museum? Or perhaps a kit of security tips for home and office produced by the nation's experts in crime prevention, the National Crime Prevention Council? Once you start doing your premium shopping at nonprofit agencies, you've got a wide-open field for finding a truly unique product—and usually at a very reasonable price.

If you're engaging in a strategic alliance to increase customer loyalty and sales, then offering a premium item as part of your campaign makes lots of sense. The premium gives consumers a lasting reminder of your partnership. Purchasing the premium provides them an extra way to support the cause. And it also gives them one more way to do business with your company, strengthening your relationship with them.

The Power of Premiums, Nonprofit-Style

Purchasing premiums from nonprofits has clear benefits for corporations:

> It gives your company a unique product, strongly differentiated from the competition's.

> It gives you a product tailored to your needs, rather than a generic product off a supply-house shelf.

> It gives you a product that meets the needs of your target market and is therefore an effective business-building tool.

> It gives you a product that is credible, creative, and associated with a worthy cause, strengthening your corporation's image.

The strategy has equally clear benefits for nonprofits:

> It enables them to reach a much larger audience with their message than they would ever reach on their own.

> It provides unrestricted operating cash.

> It pays them to do what they do best: create educational products that carry out their mission.

> It allows them to launch new product lines that can continue long after the promotion ends.

A Little Premium Can Go a Long Way
Thresher Stores and Radio Lollipop

The recent example of Thresher stores shows how minimal the premium can be and still make a huge impact. Thresher engaged in a strategic alliance with Radio Lollipop, the British-based international nonprofit that runs volunteer radio stations in children's hospitals. Thresher donated five pence per purchase to Radio Lollipop, and customers received a branded plastic bag in which they could carry the wine and spirits they purchased. A small gesture with a big return: the campaign raised £500,000 for Radio Lollipop.

Increase the Life of Your Strategic Alliance Campaign
Georgia-Pacific and the World Wildlife Fund

Georgia-Pacific, maker of MD toilet tissues, carried out a combined CRM and premium campaign with the World Wildlife Fund. In national ads, MD advertised its support of the WWF's mission and invited consumers to help support the fund by redeeming a cents-off coupon. In a conventional CRM campaign, Georgia-Pacific gave five cents to the WWF for every coupon redeemed, up to a ceiling of $20,000. But then the manufacturer added a twist: with two proofs-of-purchase from MD tissues and $11.15, consumers could purchase a WWF plush toy at a savings of seven to ten dollars. For each toy purchased, Georgia-Pacific promised to send one dollar to the World Wildlife Fund.

Adding the premium enhanced the campaign in several ways. It promoted sales of the product by providing an additional incentive to buy. It provided additional income to the WWF, which first sold the plush toys to Georgia-Pacific and then collected one dollar per toy ordered. And it put the WWF message into every home, on a tag attached to the toy.

Using Premiums as Part of a Multi-Layered CRM Campaign
Texize and McGruff the Crime Dog

How can a crime-fighting dog increase sales of home cleaning products? Just ask the Texize Division of Dow Consumer Products (now Dow Brands in Indianapolis). They teamed up with the National Crime Prevention Council (NCPC) to develop premium items to increase orders by retailers. But when Texize tossed in a CRM campaign and a strategy to benefit local retailers, they ended up having their best quarter ever!

NCPC had developed a McGruff Drug Prevention and Personal Protection curriculum for elementary school students. The curriculum used NCPC's well-known crime dog, McGruff, to teach kids how to protect themselves from crime. In a national campaign, Texize advertised that for every 200 cases of its products ordered by a store, the company would donate a one grade McGruff curriculum package to a school of the retailer's choice. For every 1,000 cases bought, Texize would donate a curriculum package for the entire school.

Texize also made a shortened version of the curriculum available to parents as a self-liquidating premium. The company purchased McGruff hand puppets and audiotapes from NCPC and offered them to parents for $4.99 and one proof-of-purchase seal from any Texize product. Simultaneously, the company ran a conventional CRM coupon campaign in which they donated twenty cents to NCPC for every coupon redeemed.

The results of the tripartite campaign were staggering. NCPC received more than $200,000 in donations and reached millions of children and families with its crime prevention message. And as we mentioned earlier, Texize experienced its best quarter ever.

8

"At the end of the day it's the power of the panda that counts. The World Wildlife Fund's famous symbol... has been used to do everything from creating awareness and building brand loyalty to encouraging trial and increasing sales."

> —Business Sponsorship of the Environment
> a publication of the World Wildlife Fund

<   <   <   <

It's a small step from sourcing your premiums from a nonprofit to licensing the nonprofit's equity for entire product lines.

And if you don't believe licensing a nonprofit can make you rich, we have two words for you: *Sesame Street.*

Licensing partnerships between nonprofits and corporations are hardly new. Universities have been doing it for decades, licensing manufacturers of pennants, jackets, mugs, and other paraphernalia to produce products bearing the university insignia. Large associations such as trade unions and professional groups have also licensed the manufacturing of products, primarily for their members. However, over the last decade the number of licensing deals has grown as both corporations and nonprofits have recognized the income-generating potential of nonprofit names, logos, and properties.

A licensing agreement is a relatively simple way of purchasing the nonprofit's name or logo to place on your product. The nonprofit, as owner of the logo, is the licensor. You are the licensee. In exchange for the use of the logo on a designated product for a designated period, you pay the nonprofit a royalty, a percentage of the price of every product sold. Most companies use licensing agents to find partners and work out the details of the agreement, although some larger companies that do a great deal of licensing handle it internally. And in most cases, licensors will also have the right to approve any use of their identity, to ensure that their equity is not tarnished or misused.

Companies have used licensing arrangements with nonprofits to meet a variety of needs.

Attracting a Target Market
Parents, Kids, and Sesame Street

Licensing a product from a nonprofit enables you to attract that organization's market.

The best example is the ubiquitous *Sesame Street*. If you've ever wandered the aisles of Toys "R" Us, you know you can't go far without running into Big Bird, Ernie, and the rest of the gang from the popular television show. *Sesame Street* is still going strong after decades. (Can you say, "Tickle Me Elmo"?) Lunchboxes, clothing, dolls, school supplies, room decorations... the list goes on and on. Each of those images has been licensed from Children's Television Workshop, the nonprofit organization that produces the show. And each has turned an otherwise undistinguished item into a must-have for millions of *Sesame Street* fans. And why not? In an age when cartoons are sometimes just extended advertisements for product lines, it's refreshing to be able to buy a product from a company that has its heart in the right place... and still know that your kids will love it.

Repositioning a Product
Cadbury and the World Wildlife Fund

Tying a product to a nonprofit through licensing can be an effective way to reposition an otherwise undistinguished performer, by giving it an identity that makes it stand out from the crowd.

For example, Cadbury, the British chocolate maker, wanted to increase the sales of its twenty-gram chocolate bar. Market research had shown that the target market liked animals and was interested in animal causes. So Cadbury approached the World Wildlife Fund. In a licensing agreement with the fund, Cadbury repositioned the bar as the Cadbury Wildlife Bar, placing the WWF logo on the wrapper and paying a royalty to the organization for every bar sold. Sales increased by 35 percent in the first year.

More Licensing that's Good Enough to Eat
The World Wildlife Fund, Zeelandia Bread, and Lyons Maid Ice Cream

We're trying not to turn this chapter into an advertisement for the World Wildlife Fund, but it's not easy. The WWF has a proven history of helping their corporate partners in a wide variety of areas.

When Zeelandia Bread, a Dutch bakery, wanted to launch a new line of bread, they partnered with the WWF to produce Panda Broodje, or Panda Bread. Packaging carried a picture of the Panda, the WWF's symbol, and point-of-sale material included pins, flags, and tiny stuffed Pandas. According to H.J. Doeleman, Director of General Zeelandia Holland, "We were able to sell through 85 percent of Dutch bakers, an extremely high proportion in a competitive industry. It is amazing that we were able to achieve such a wide distribution so quickly."

Lyons Maid Ice Cream, a division of Allied Lyons UK, recently launched Panda Vanilla and Chocolate Ice Cream Lollies in a promotion with the WWF. According to the Product Manager, Alistair Allen, the sales forces were so "extremely motivated by the knowledge that their efforts would help the WWF" that the new brand performed 15 percent better than the other lines during the promotional period.

Licensing Expertise
Columbia University

Ever since the passage of the Dole-Bayh Bill in 1981, universities have been authorized to hold patent and licensing rights to discoveries produced with federal funding. Like the Oklahoma Land Rush, institutions have been racing to seize the new sources of funding. From medical schools to MBA programs, students work on projects for their own advancement that also net fees or donations from the private sector. In fact, without medical schools, the pharmaceutical industry's cost structures would be radically different. Research grants are a low cost way of buying the expertise of entire groups of individuals who, in a few years, would require higher salaries as employees.

Columbia University in New York is a prime example. Between the late 1980s and early 1990s, annual revenues from licenses and patents have risen from roughly $4 million to approximately $24 million. Universities are now aggressively seeking partnerships with private business to exploit university research. At Columbia, for example, the School of Engineering has engaged in materials testing for the private sector, providing experience and learning opportunities for its graduate students while bringing in large amounts of capital through fees.

Licensing Goodwill

Share Our Strength Licensing Partners

Share Our Strength (SOS) is most famous for working with American Express on Taste of the Nation and the Charge Against Hunger. But some of the funding for their anti-hunger and anti-poverty efforts comes from licensing their name to corporate partners in return for royalties. The SOS logo appears on several pans produced by Calphalon Cookware in return for a percentage of pan sales. Share Our Strength has also partnered with both Fetzer Vineyards and E&J Gallo Winery, who sell cases of wine carrying the SOS logo in return for a per case donation. And Cains Foods produces a line of food products named for Share Our Strength's Taste of the Nation anti-hunger benefit.

How Nonprofits See Licensing Agreements

Of all the forms of strategic partnerships, licensing is the one that nonprofits have been the slowest to embrace. Nonprofits have mixed responses to licensing, but they have good reason to be wary. On the one hand, they want to license their equity because they want the benefits it can bring in terms of money and exposure. On the other hand, several factors argue against it.

One caution is the nonprofit's ever-vigilant concern with integrity. If a nonprofit sells its name and logo to a corporation, will it be perceived as too commercial? Will it tarnish its image as a trustworthy doer of good deeds? This concern is real and must be addressed by anyone who wants to license a nonprofit trademark. The way to address it is to license a nonprofit's name only for a product that genuinely promotes its mission.

A second concern is image. How will the nonprofit's name be used? Will it have any control? Will the product reflect the quality of the organization? These concerns are no different from those of a corporate licensor, so address that concern the same way you would with a corporate partner. Assure the nonprofit that the product will be first-class and then follow through. The reason you're dealing with them is because of who they are in the world. You wouldn't want to kill the goose that lays the golden eggs, would you?

A third reason that nonprofits are wary of licensing is concern about their time and energy. They fear that engaging in licensing will divert them from their primary purpose. You can address this concern by helping your potential partner analyze the pros and cons of the program. How much time will it take to administer? Will the nonprofit need to add a staff person? Will the royalties it collects more than cover its time and expense? Performing a program analysis together can be a useful educational process for both partners and can help you build a good working relationship.

A fourth reason that some nonprofits are slow to embrace licensing has to do with the nonprofit culture, which does not lend itself to seeking—or seeing—licensing opportunities in its midst. Staff members focus on carrying out their mission, not on making money from it. As a result, licensing is a concept most nonprofits have simply never considered, and your prospective nonprofit partner may need some wooing. You may need to gradually cultivate the nonprofit's interest in the program, meeting with key executives and board members several times to educate them about the benefits licensing can bring. (We suggest giving them a copy of our first book, *Filthy Rich and Other Nonprofit Fantasies*. If that doesn't whet their appetite, nothing will.)

It may help them to know that nonprofits that have entered into licensing agreements have been extremely pleased with the results. They've found the increased exposure and the increased cash flow well worth the time spent developing and managing the program. It is entirely likely that as nonprofit enterprise grows in popularity, more and more organizations will discover the benefits of licensing and become eager to take part.

Licensing General Rules

If you decide to pursue licensing with a nonprofit partner, keep the following guidelines in mind:

> Make sure there is a logical relationship between the nonprofit and the product: don't force a connection just to get an appealing name on your product. The public won't buy it. Sales will suffer. So may the reputation of the nonprofit.

> Make sure the product needs to exist. Don't create a product just for the sake of putting a nonprofit's name on it. If the market doesn't need and want it, even the best name won't make it sell.

> Make sure the corporation and the nonprofit agree on the terms of the deal and the product before you begin. Differences are easier to iron out before production than after.

9

VENDOR RELATIONSHIPS

"This flavor combines our super creamy vanilla ice cream with chunks of Rainforest Crunch, a new cashew and Brazilian nut butter crunch. Money from the purchase of these nuts will help Brazilian forest peoples start a nut shelling cooperative that they'll own and operate. Rainforest Crunch helps to show that the rainforests are more profitable when their nuts, fruits, and medicinal plants are cultivated for traditional harvest than when their trees are cut for short-term gain."
—*message on Ben & Jerry's Rainforest Crunch ice cream carton*

<   <   <   <

You may remember reading this message while scarfing down spoonfuls of Ben & Jerry's Rainforest Crunch. If so, the notion of buying products to benefit a cause will be familiar to you. If not, the idea may seem a bit unorthodox. Companies like Ben & Jerry's and The Body Shop buy products to benefit causes because they know that buying from nonprofits benefits themselves as well. Surprisingly, nonprofit vendors can be less expensive than for-profit equivalents, because they have different cost structures. They may even be the only place you can get the product or service.

These days, nonprofits sell their expertise just like for-profit businesses do. American Express "buys" the expertise of Share Our Strength to administer their hunger programs. Dance companies sell performances (and sometimes classes). Counseling centers sell therapy. Environmental organizations sell information and services to protect the environment. Economic development groups sell services to rebuild inner cities. Job training centers sell the labor of their trainees. The range of products and services is as large as the number of fields in which nonprofits operate—which is to say it is virtually limitless.

Chances are, many of the products and services you now purchase from for-profit suppliers could also be purchased from nonprofit organizations.

For instance, to produce its Chocolate Fudge Brownie ice cream and low fat frozen yogurt, Ben & Jerry's needs brownies. A lot of them. (In 1997, they bought $2,705,000 worth of brownies.) Since 1988, they have been buying those brownies from Greyston Bakery in Yonkers, New York. The bakery is run by the Greyston Foundation, a nonprofit social service network that provides employment, training, child care, and other services to the low-income community where it's located. As anyone who's ever tasted Chocolate Fudge Brownie can tell you, those brownies made by homeless and low-income workers taste just as good as any other brownies. But knowing you're helping those workers learn a trade and become self-sufficient may make them easier to swallow.

Now, we're not recommending that you switch all, or even most, of your vendor business to nonprofit suppliers. We're merely saying that doing business with a nonprofit is possible. It is also sometimes beneficial, because buying from a nonprofit can provide many of the same benefits that come with other forms of strategic alliances. For instance:

> Unlike goods from a for-profit supplier, a nonprofit's offerings come factory-loaded with goodwill, which rubs off on your business.

> Nonprofits are experts in their fields. In fact, they are often the most qualified sources of information or expertise in their area. So if you're looking for an authority in a particular field, try a nonprofit.

> Nonprofits pack credibility. If you want to offer a product or service that inspires confidence, a nonprofit may be your best supplier.

> Nonprofits can offer access to new markets. If you want to reach a target market, try products from nonprofits which serve that audience.

> Nonprofits can tailor products and services to your needs. Unlike a commercial supplier, which supplies the same product or service to

multiple clients, a nonprofit is likely to develop a unique relationship with you, designing a customized product or service to meet your needs and its own.

> And, of course, nonprofits need the income and exposure that can come from selling their products and services to corporations. If you buy a product or service from a nonprofit, you know that you're helping it achieve its mission.

Vendor relationships with nonprofits run the gamut from very sophisticated to very simple. They can be long-term arrangements or short-term contracts. The following examples show the range of products and services nonprofits provide and the range of corporate needs they are hired to meet.

Finding New Products
Merck and the Costa Rican Rainforest

New product development is the lifeblood of any company that aspires to be more than a one hit wonder, but it can be one of the most costly aspects of doing business. Partnership with a nonprofit can open the doors to new product lines at a far lower cost than R&D or even the acquisition of an undervalued competitor (the strategy with which Harold Geneen built ITT). Merck is hoping their strategic partnership in the Costa Rican rainforest will sprout new products—and huge profits.

Merck is one of the world's largest pharmaceutical companies, with a strong sense of self-interest in developing new drugs from previously unknown sources. One of these sources is Costa Rica's National Institute of Biodiversity (INBio). In a partnership with Merck, INBio collects a wide range of plants and insects that may have the potential of becoming new medicines. They supply Merck with the specimens, and if any product is developed from those samples, then Merck donates to the National Parks System and INBio. In addition, Merck provides direct support for conservation of the rainforests and its scientific team provides training for local scientists.

Socially Responsible Product Sourcing
The Body Shop's Community Trade Program

The Body Shop International and Anita Roddick, its founder, are pioneers in the area of supporting "long-term sustainable trading relationships with communities in need." In 1994 the Body Shop International developed guidelines for Community Trade partnerships. Since then, they have doubled their suppliers. In fiscal year 1996/1997 they bought £826,425 worth of raw materials and accessories from twenty-two Community Trade suppliers. Some of these suppliers are nonprofits, like CORR-The Jute Works, a women's nonprofit handicraft marketing trust in Bangladesh. And some are for-profit groups that support their communities through charitable foundations. One of these is Teddy Exports, makers of wooden massage items in Madurai, India. Through it's charitable foundation, The Teddy Trust, they run a school, various AIDS awareness initiatives, and health, education, and veterinary services for employees and the local community. In one instance, The Body Shop not only buys products from a supplier, but also pays an extra premium to fund social programs. When The Body Shop buys hand-made paper products from General Paper Industries in Nepal, they pay an extra premium above the agreed upon price to fund the General Welfare Pratishtan, an independent trust to help the community in matters of health, education, and the environment.

Providing a Needed Service
American Express and Share Our Strength

American Express decided to make hunger relief a beneficiary of their corporate philanthropy, but they realized they needed help evaluating requests for funding support.

Enter Share Our Strength. A world leader in the area of hunger relief, they were the perfect partner for a joint venture with AmEx. Since 1984 SOS has distributed over $50 million to over 1,000 anti-hunger and anti-poverty organizations. They had a better base of knowledge to evaluate funding requests, and they could use as much corporate help themselves as they could get. The result has been one of the leading CRM partnership efforts in the world, with American Express raising millions of dollars each year and Share Our Strength directing those funds to worthy organizations around the world.

Their relationship includes American Express' primary sponsorship of Taste of the Nation, a national anti-hunger benefit run by Share Our Strength since 1987. As of their tenth anniversary in 1997, Taste of the Nation events had raised more than $27.8 million. Other sponsors include Calphalon and Evian.

10

EMPLOYEE VOLUNTEERING

*"Much too often, nonprofit organizations serving the community have more
work than staff or money. In such cases, these groups may find themselves
with extremely worthwhile projects that cannot be completed because of a
lack of personnel."*

—*from "Community Service at IBM"*

<   <   <   <

What's a person worth? In terms of chemicals, not very much (the latest esti-
mate was around $4.95). But in terms of experience, education, capability,
effort, and passion, a person can be priceless.

That's why one of the most important gifts a corporation can give to nonprofits is people—corporate employees as volunteers. Nonprofits rely on volunteers to carry out many of their programs and they rarely have enough, so
the arrival of a motivated, committed crew of workers can be as good as cash.

They're also cheaper for your company to give away than money. Not only
do you get them back, but for the most part, any minor costs associated are
more than outweighed by the benefits in additional experience, job satisfaction, and employee morale. There's even good news on the legal front: since
the passage of the Volunteer Protection Act of 1997, charity volunteers are pro-
tected from being held legally liable for accidents that happen in connection
with their nonprofit work.

Volunteering can help you grab the public eye. When Lucent
Technologies launched the Lucent Foundation, they did it with a Global Day
of Caring in October 1996. Nearly 5,800 employees volunteered approximately 26,000 hours for causes around the world, from building homes with
Habitat for Humanity to wiring schools to the Internet to cleaning up the envi-

ronment. The day was meant to show the company's commitment to social responsibility, and it did exactly that. It's not surprising that Lucent would understand the appropriate use of volunteers: it's connected to the Pioneer Group, the largest private volunteer group in the U.S., made up of employees from former Bell companies.

In 1998, in celebration of its 75th anniversary, the Walt Disney Company sponsored a weekend of worldwide volunteerism. More than 17,000 participated in the Disney VoluntEars Global Celebration of Children in twenty countries on five continents.

Peter Drucker—the respected author, management consultant, and college professor—suggests that companies use employee volunteer programs as tools for management training, because they help employees hone their skills in managing and motivating people. Companies with active volunteer programs find their employees enjoy the opportunity to give time to an organization. They like the feeling of contributing to society and return to work motivated and refreshed.

Participating in a corporate volunteer program also makes employees feel good about the company. Surveys like Cone/Roper and MORI have shown that employees prefer to work for companies that participate in community service. The knowledge that a company cares tends to inspire loyalty and pride.

The trend is so popular that some nonprofits are even marketing themselves to corporations as service providers. New York Cares offers corporate partners turnkey programs that involve their employees in community service. The programs operate on three levels: four large scale Annual Service Events, over two thousand year-round Hands-On Service and customized programs, and Philanthropic Giving and CRM. For interested corporations, New York Cares assigns a corporate relations manager to discuss objectives and get the ball rolling.

Donating your employees can have unexpected benefits for your company, as IBM Deutschland discovered. They lent executives to the German government to devise a computer-based pollution monitoring system for the Elbe River. Not only did the employees develop new skills, they used those skills to create a new software product that IBM was able to sell around the globe.

The huge British retailer, Marks & Spencer, lends up to thirty executives a year to nonprofit and public sector projects. They call the program "seconding" and the moves are often seen as personal or career development initiatives. Many of the executives are younger employees, "seconded" with the intention of helping them learn and grow.

Corporate volunteers run the gamut from skilled to unskilled, short-term to long-term. They include people from every level of a corporation, working independently or in teams. Although most companies urge employees to volunteer their own time, many let workers help nonprofits on the company clock. In short, the rules governing employee volunteer programs are as diverse as the companies that run them. Only three general rules seem to guide the successful ones:

1. Let employees drive the program.

2. Let them pick the agencies they will serve.

3. Be sincere—commit to the program, talk about it in company newsletters, help employees find agencies to work for, recognize volunteers.

The following programs have been chosen to illustrate the range of possibilities:

One Person Can Make a Difference... And It Adds Up
From Home Depot to Team Depot

"When we opened our first Home Depot store in 1979, we began with the premise that one person can make a difference. We have held fast to that notion for sixteen years, and now with 80,000 associates..." Home Depot's Social Responsibility Report for 1995 is filled with tales of small contributions at local levels, stories of individual volunteers who made a difference, and larger, national co-ventures with groups like the March of Dimes Birth Defects Foundation. From the first page to the last, the image that comes across is that of Home Depot changing the world through volunteerism. They call their force Team Depot, and it's an award-winning, community-minded juggernaut of involvement.

A prime example took place at a Home Depot near Fort Bragg in Fayetteville, North Carolina, in 1995. Home Depot associate Mikie Hoeye planned a series of clinics to teach Army wives how to handle simple home repair tasks if their spouses were deployed. Mikie, an Army spouse herself, partnered with U.S. Army family support units to teach classes in lawn care, budget decorating, and tiling. "When I began these clinics I didn't know if we would be sending troops to Bosnia. I was glad to help customers who all of a sudden were faced with the sole responsibility of taking care of their homes and families."

Another example: Even though their new store had been open less than a month, Team Depot volunteers from the Whitby, Ontario, stores joined the Red Cross in cleaning up dangerous debris when a tornado ravaged the nearby community of Bridgenorth, Ontario.

A bigger example: In 1995, the company received a National Team Award from the March of Dimes Birth Defects Foundation for having 450 dedicated associates in forty U.S. cities participate in their drive for healthy babies.

The report includes a partial list of their funded organizations that numbers just under 350, and information on applying for a grant or recruiting Team Depot volunteers. In other words, not only does Home Depot want to make sure you understand that their corporate identity springs from their social responsibility and volunteerism, but they also want to help you, too.

A Team Approach to Volunteering

Target Stores and the Good Neighbor Program

Target Stores has a strong commitment to making its communities healthy places in which to live and raise a family. One of the ways Target Stores expresses that commitment is by actively encouraging employee volunteers. The Good Neighbor Program, administered from the company's corporate headquarters in Minneapolis as part of its corporate giving program, has an annual budget of $250,000, which is spent to support employee volunteer efforts in each of the company's locations. In 1996, employees and their families contributed over 168,000 hours of community service.

The Good Neighbor Program emphasizes the use of teams of Target employees to solve community problems. Local employees choose the cause. Projects range from the March of Dimes Walk America pledge drive, to

"Paint-a-thons" in which teams paint the houses of the elderly, to "Adopt-a-School" programs in which teams of workers tutor children, organize carnivals, chaperone field trips, and build playground equipment. Joint efforts include Meals-on-Wheels, Special Olympics, Big Brothers/Big Sisters, and Boy Scouts/Girl Scouts. Employees do their volunteering on their own time. Headquarters urges each Target location to do at least one volunteer project a year. Virtually every location participates. Some do the bare minimum, most do more. Some do as many as fifty projects.

Target believes employee management is important—and educational. Volunteer Good Neighbor Captains must locate community projects, coordinate frequently conflicting employee desires, and manage volunteer supplies and schedules. Headquarters lets captains make arrangements on company time. It also gives them a Good Neighbor Guidebook that contains everything a captain needs to know. Headquarters tracks the efforts of its volunteers and disseminates stories of successful volunteer efforts.

Why does Target require teamwork rather than individual volunteering? In mercenary terms, Target wants the maximum return for their investment. The company believes that by working together, employees build a spirit of teamwork that carries over into the workplace. The company also believes that by sending teams of Target workers out into the community, it builds the company's presence there. Teams of Target workers, all wearing Target t-shirts, make a strong statement that Target Stores cares about its neighbors.

Forging an International Corporate Culture through Volunteerism
Electronic Data Systems and Global Volunteer Day

Electronic Data Systems (EDS) is a rapidly growing multinational corporation with more than 80,000 employees in forty countries. Volunteerism is one of their key areas of corporate contributions. And while they pursue volunteerism on a local level wherever they have divisions, Global Volunteer Day is where EDS really shines.

On an international scale, EDS holds an annual Global Volunteer Day. The first one was in 1993 and involved 10,000 participants. The next year, 20,000 took part. In 1997 EDS employees volunteered nearly 50,000 hours on 386 projects in 200 locations in thirty-two countries. The goal of Global Volunteer Day is to promote an international image of good corporate citizenship. But it has other results. According to EDS, their work touches the lives of over one million people.

Countries where volunteerism is not part of the culture, such as in Asia and the Pacific, were at first confused by the idea. In New Zealand, where EDS finished acquiring a bank just a week before Global Volunteer Day, 30 percent of the bank's employees still took part in eleven different projects. According to Susan Smith, EDS's manager of corporate philanthropy, "Global Volunteer Day serves to announce us in the community." She added that in New Zealand people "were flabbergasted that a company would do this."

11

IN-KIND DONATIONS

"We at L'eggs Products Inc., have certainly realized what a smart investment in-kind giving is. Over the past few years, it has helped us trim inventory, increase productivity, free warehouse space, and subsequently reduce the cost of storing inventory."

—*L'eggs Products Inc.*

Okay, let's put on our bean counter hats for this chapter.

Financial shenanigans aside, a one dollar donation costs your company one dollar. But one dollar worth of product rarely costs one dollar.

So which would you rather give away? Money or product?

The list of "donatables" is long. It includes products in current inventory as well as ones that would otherwise be liquidated or thrown away. It includes services companies perform as their major line of business, as well as services they perform for their own use.

If the list of things a company can donate to a nonprofit is long, so is the list of reasons for doing so:

> First, there are tax benefits. Companies that donate used products can often deduct the fair market value of the items. Companies that donate current unsold inventory can deduct even more. They can take a "stepped up" deduction, which equals the cost of making the product plus half the difference between its cost and its retail price (up to twice the cost). For example, if you donate an item that cost $50 to manufacture and sells for $100, you can deduct $75.

> Second, there are inventory control benefits. Donating products can save your company warehousing costs as well as inventory carrying costs and can help you dispose of out-of-date products without destroying or liquidating them.

> Third, there are public relations benefits. As with any other type of cause-related marketing, donations can be made strategically—to groups in your geographic area, for instance, or to certain types of agencies. In this way they can be used to reinforce marketing goals. For instance, in Seattle, the home base of Microsoft, contributions from the high-tech industry have doubled in a five-year period to $7 million in 1996. But that's just the local market. In August, 1997 Microsoft alone gave $200 million in software, training and equipment for an electronic information access program for public libraries. Oracle announced a $100 million donation of software for schools.

> Fourth, there are philanthropic benefits. Giving products to a nonprofit helps it do its work—sometimes even more than an equivalent amount of cash.

The following stories describe a variety of in-kind donation programs and the benefits they bring to the nonprofit recipients and their corporate donors.

Donating Current Inventory
Home Depot and Kids Can't Fly

In a well-designed, in-kind joint venture, the numbers don't have to be huge to be significant. In 1995 Home Depot took part in "Kids Can't Fly," a public information campaign aimed at educating parents in the Boston area about the dangers of open windows. Home Depot partnered with local government to provide specially designed window guards aimed at keeping children from falling, donating 500 of the guards to needy families. The program was highly successful, reducing injuries by 77 percent. For the price of 500 window guards, Home Depot purchased an amazing level of good will and consumer loyalty.

Donating Products and Services

Filter Queen and the National Trust for Historic Preservation

At first glance, some strategic relationships may seem unusual, or even unnecessary. But in the case of Filter Queen and the National Trust for Historic Preservation, it couldn't make more sense for either of the parties involved.

Filter Queen is a Cleveland-based manufacturer of home filtration and cleaning equipment with annual revenues of $40-50 million. In their first national-scale philanthropic endeavor, they decided to partner with the National Trust for Historic Preservation. Filter Queen has pledged $1.3 million in products, services, cash and promotional support to help preserve historic homes. Plus a portion of profits from every sale goes to the Trust.

How did this unusual alliance come to exist? According to Gary Moore, the president of Filter Queen's parent company, "Our company's core competency is in the filtration business—making things last. Most of the deterioration that goes on in homes is from dust and dirt... We like to think we have a corporate soul, and we like to give back as much as we get."

Their decision to support the Trust comes at the perfect time—the Trust's government funding was ending this year. In return for the donations, Filter Queen is running a national promotional campaign using historic homes and outlining the role of the National Trust and Filter Queen products in preserving the home. According to Moore, "It does an awful lot for our distribution network in the local communities." With more than 250 distributors nationwide, that can have a serious impact on Filter Queen's market share.

Donating Waste Products

New Covent Garden Soup Company, Starbuck's, Hewlett-Packard,
and ZooPoo

Some nonprofits virtually owe their existence to corporate waste. This is especially true for food banks, which receive a portion of their foodstuffs from individuals, but get the lion's share from food processors and retailers. Most of the food donated is mislabeled or otherwise improperly packaged. It may be unfit for commercial sale, but it feeds programs for hungry and homeless people nationwide. As we mentioned earlier, New Covent Garden Soup Company began its relationship with Crisis because they were looking for someone to take their surplus inventory off their hands. Starbuck's Coffee, with headquarters in Seattle, prides itself on selling only the freshest beans. It gives its older beans to local food banks, which are happy to serve the classy brew to their clients.

For the majority of nonprofits, office equipment and supplies top the list of desirable gifts. Many nonprofits still slug out memos on electric typewriters. Donations of older but usable computers, calculators, office furniture and other equipment can save them hours of labor and hundreds or thousands of dollars.

In Englewood, Colorado, a Hewlett-Packard sales office was able to find a way to use the Styrofoam peanuts that come with their products. They donate them to local Boy Scouts, who sell them to Mail Boxes Etc. and other companies. The profit goes for scholarships to send needy boys to the Scout's summer camp.

Last but not least is what we think is the ultimate donation of waste products. Twenty years ago the Bronx Frontier, a nonprofit community-based organization started an earned income venture that turned poop into profit. They made a deal with the Bronx Zoo to remove and package animal manure and sell it as fertilizer—called Zoo Doo—in the Bloomingdale's Christmas Catalog. The fertile idea was a hit, selling 30,000 bags that year. The idea is going strong today, catching on with zoos around the world. In Perth, Australia, they call it ZooPoo.

Donating Space
Home Depot and Hurricane Opal

Home Depot's employee volunteers, Team Depot, make responding to disaster a high priority. Especially when sharing available resources can make a critical difference to the community. When Hurricane Hugo hit the Florida Panhandle, Georgia, and Alabama in 1995, Team Depot was there. They donated the use of their 70,000 square-foot warehouse in Dacula, Georgia, to be used by the American Red Cross as a distribution hub.

Donating Cyberspace
CNN, IBM, and the American Red Cross

In the high-tech version of what Home Depot did, CNN and IBM have joined together with the American Red Cross to create a disaster information Web site. IBM donated technical expertise and $1.5 million in computer equipment. CNN is donating the Internet access and also links to their news service. The Red Cross will provide up-to-the-minute, disaster-related information from the sites. The Web site tells disaster victims how to obtain food, shelter, clothing, and counseling, and tells Web surfers how they can help or make a donation.

Building a New Market with In-Kind Donations
BellSouth Wires Schools to the Internet

Sometimes you have to build a market before you can own it. That's just what BellSouth is doing in the Southeast United States.

Beginning in 1996, the telecommunications company embarked upon an effort to provide Internet access and training to approximately 4,000 schools in its nine-state operating area. In the process, BellSouth will make a difference in the lives of two million students and 172,000 teachers. The program includes the installation of an entire infrastructure, from wiring and computers to support materials and teacher training. It also includes free Internet access for students, teachers, and school staffs. In an attempt to make the entire project turnkey, BellSouth has covered every aspect of the program, so everybody gets everything BellSouth promised with no hidden gaps or extra charges. In addition to 5,400 employee volunteers, BellSouth has involved one of its suppliers, Lucent Technologies.

What does BellSouth hope to gain?

They get market penetration. BellSouth technology is deployed throughout the entire operating area. They also get goodwill, name recognition, supplier and customer involvement, and an investment in the future of their customer base. Most of BellSouth's commitment was in-kind donation of equipment, network access time, and employees.

Was it philanthropic? Sure. Was it profitable? Time will tell. But how much would you pay to be where they are right now?

Clearinghouses for In-Kind Donations
Gifts In Kind America and the NAEIR

Companies that want to donate products to a nonprofit, but don't want the hassle of administering a program, can use a clearinghouse. Gifts In Kind America and the National Association for the Exchange of Industrial Resources (NAEIR) are just two organizations that provide this service.

Both nonprofits develop giving programs for companies on a turnkey basis. Together they help approximately two thousand companies a year donate current inventory to nonprofit organizations. They donate software packages for Microsoft, shoes for Nike, clothing for K Mart, personal care products for Gillette, and other products for other Fortune 500 and smaller companies. Gifts In Kind has been around since 1984—in 1996, they distributed over $204 million goods and services. NAEIR, which has been around since 1977, distributed over $90 million in 1996.

Some donations represent excess inventory, a one-time surplus a company needs to dispose of. Other items are part of a long-term giving program of corporations that are administered by the clearinghouse. The companies refer requests for donations directly to the clearinghouse, which processes the requests, arranges the shipping, provides the required tax documentation, and even handles the publicity. This turnkey service is free to the corporate donors. Costs are covered by the nonprofit recipients, who pay shipping and handling fees as well as a yearly membership fee. Gifts In Kind America also receives donations from United Way and foundations.

12

"We view philanthropy as an investment, a strategic asset that requires the same level of disciplined processes and evaluation as any other aspect of the business."

—*Jeff Krause*
Director
GM Philanthropic Administration

<   <   <   <

Some people tend to think that strategic philanthropy is tainted in a way that "pure" philanthropy is not. That it's dishonest because it has an ulterior motive. Even, surprisingly, that it's a recent invention. But in fact the practice of using philanthropic dollars to buy benefits for a company dates back at least to the 1860s.

The beneficiary of the earliest strategic philanthropy was the YMCA. The benefactors were America's railroad barons. They were the primary supporters of the YMCA, not because they believed in its programs, but because they needed cheap housing for their railroad crews. They saw the benefit of serving the community and their business interests with one project.

Many people would be surprised to know that until 1954 corporate law mandated that a company's donations must directly benefit its stockholders. In 1954 a New Jersey Supreme Court ruled that a publicly-held business could make charitable contributions that did not produce income for stockholders. For the next three decades, corporations set a new trend in giving, donating to organizations with no apparent connection to their businesses, to avoid the appearance of greed.

Corporations still spent their money strategically, but after 1954 they spent more of it on community programs. These expenditures served two purposes. They strengthened community resources, making the local community a better place to recruit employees, raise families, and do business. Equally important, they earned the goodwill of employees, customers, and government officials.

Some companies refined the process, spending philanthropic dollars on cultural events with specifically targeted payoffs. A perfect example of this happened when United Technologies wanted to build its business in the Middle East. They sponsored a Smithsonian exhibition of Islamic Art. The exhibition built important contacts for the company in Saudi Arabia, facilitating their entry into that market. Another less obvious example is Texaco's sponsorship of the Metropolitan Opera since 1940 (even before the 1954 ruling). Why would an oil company sponsor an opera? Because Texaco has over twice its normal market share among motorists who regularly listen to opera.

Now tighter budgets have put increased pressure on corporations to justify expenditures. If contributions can be targeted to causes that help the bottom line, so much the better: they're easier to sell to management and to shareholders, while still achieving their philanthropic goals.

New Goals for Giving

What are the targets that help the bottom line? Where are business leaders spending their money, and what can we learn from how they're spending it?

Companies can always justify spending money on new business development, so it's no surprise that philanthropic dollars end up there. The same with marketing, where it's easy to spend money on reinforcing image and customer loyalty. The biggest surprise might be human resources, which is frequently under-funded and could use the help.

New Business Development

We've just mentioned how United Technologies used philanthropic dollars to open markets in the Middle East. They did the same thing when they wanted to cement their position as a leading aerospace company doing business in France. They sponsored another Smithsonian exhibition, on French landscape painting, which opened at the National Gallery in Washington,

D.C., then moved to Paris, where the opening was attended by officials of the French government who were in a position to help the company.

Another way to spend your company's money is the way the Bristol-Myers Squibb Foundation does. Like most drug company foundations, they give money to universities to support unrestricted biomedical research that may eventually benefit the company.

Marketing

Image building has always been a favorite use of philanthropic dollars. Mobil has been sponsoring public television for years because it strengthened their image with educated consumers. The sponsorship did such a good job building Mobil's image, they even got letters thanking them for sponsoring a PBS Shakespeare series that was actually sponsored by their competitor.

> One of the most famous examples of image building and inspiring customer loyalty has to be the Ronald McDonald Houses. McDonald's has gained worldwide notoriety for the centers, which provide places to stay for families of children in hospitals. It's a high-profile way to show their target markets (kids, families, communities, and the lower/middle classes) that they care. In Australia, Ronald McDonald houses have helped the golden arches stand head and shoulders above other companies. Surveys report that McDonald's is the company most associated with a cause, and that programs like the Houses are the most preferred form of corporate social involvement. Nineteen percent of Australian consumers polled based a purchase on association with a cause—of those, 30 percent were at McDonald's. (The Body Shop was second with six percent.)

> Strategic philanthropy can also be used to help build images among minorities. The Adolph Coors Company's corporate giving department has initiatives that target three consumer groups: African Americans, Hispanics, and women. Each year the company gives a predetermined amount of money to nonprofit causes that appeal to these groups, because it knows that support of minority causes will help it build business with those consumers.

Human Resources

Corporations are increasingly targeting philanthropic spending at programs that benefit their employees. They're also spending money on programs that will help create better employees in the future. Beyond making sense, the practice is also making money. Let's take a look at a few examples of how strategic philanthropy can produce serious benefits for human resources.

> The Lucent Foundation, the giving arm of Lucent Technologies, was founded at the end of 1996 with a giving budget of $18 million and another $2 million in direct corporate giving for 1997. Its first grant? Three million dollars for a program to provide training for production associates at community colleges near Lucent Technologies' manufacturing facilities.

> The Stride Rite corporation in Cambridge, Massachusetts, uses money from its corporate charitable foundation to subsidize tuition at its two on-site day care centers. The first was built in 1971, when Stride Rite became one of the earliest U.S. companies to offer on-site day care. The second in 1991, when Stride Rite became the first to offer an intergenerational center that serves both children and elderly relatives of employees. Stride Rite executives have estimated that the centers, which have received international acclaim, save the children's shoe manufacturer $22,000 per employee by helping it retain high-quality workers and avoid the cost of training replacements.

A New Game Plan, Too

Strategic philanthropy is becoming a powerful tool, so companies have fundamentally changed the way they employ it. The days of CEOs writing checks to their spouses' charities are ending, along with the days when corporate giving officers could keep their jobs without producing tangible results. Now every dollar has to pull as much weight as possible. The good news is that every dollar can pull more when the whole company is involved.

"Pure" philanthropic grant decisions were guided by society's need for programs and applicant's merit. But strategic philanthropy is about helping the causes that can help your company, so the criteria are vastly different: marketing, human resources, and new business development. A program that appeals to stakeholders (customers, employees, shareholders, and the community) is more likely to receive funds than a cause that has no benefit to your company.

In companies that practice "pure" philanthropy, the funding decisions are generally made by corporate giving staffs. Strategic givers rely on a more diverse range of players within a company. Each group brings with it a different perspective and a different take on company goals:

> Human resources is consulted about employee concerns, workforce development, and other areas that might be served by corporate gifts.

> Marketing is asked about the company's marketing goals: are there target populations that might be served through a donation?

> Public relations has input on how a gift could help the company achieve PR goals in the community.

> Community relations is asked about community problems worth targeting.

> Business development officers, government relations specialists, and shareholder relations staff may be brought in to contribute to the decision.

> Corporate giving staffs are still part of the mix, but there is serious pressure on them to produce results. The publications that serve the corporate philanthropy sector are filled with stories of corporate contributions managers who no longer have jobs because they couldn't make the transition to strategic philanthropy—and stories about the superstars who can take the ball and run with it.

Here's an example of how one global megacorp shifted from traditional philanthropy to strategic philanthropy:

> When the gigantic pharmaceutical company SmithKline Beecham wanted to change its giving program so it got more "bang for the buck", it surveyed more than 800 of its managers in the United States and United Kingdom. Their feedback about the company's social responsibility led to the creation of a corporate task force made up of ten senior executives from various markets. The task force came up with a new strategy: aligning corporate philanthropy with the company's interest while adding value globally to healthcare philanthropy. To this end the company created partnership management teams representing worldwide markets. Teams were made up of people from manufacturing, government relations, corporate relations, business strategies, legal, medical, health policy, and product management. The task force also outlined the SmithKline Beecham Community Promise: a commitment to make a difference in the standards of health where the company operates. To put some muscle behind their promise, the company increased its overall giving budget by $3.2 million to $11.2 million for 1997. By turning to its managers and executives to redefine its giving strategy, SmithKline Beecham got what a traditional corporate giving department couldn't provide: a synergistic solution that redefined who the company was in the world by unifying its philanthropic goals with its business goals.

Many strategic givers outline the goals of their gifts in measurable terms. For example: 25 percent of employees will participate, all major local media will pick up the story, half the research projects will be on subjects we pick, and so on. Some corporations carry out formal evaluations after the fact to see if their goals were met. They treat gifts like business expenses, measuring results as they would any business program. Like companies who prefer direct response ads to image ads, many corporations won't run programs whose results they can't measure.

> Church & Dwight, the maker of Arm & Hammer Baking Soda, has a system to measure the impact of their corporate giving plan. Its philanthropic projects range from developing a community-based,

youth-oriented, water resource management program to providing seed money for a major national initiative led by the National Fish and Wildlife Foundation, National 4-H Clubs, the U.S. Department of Agriculture, and the University of Wisconsin Extension Services. Regardless of the program, Church & Dwight knows the full range of results it yielded. The company's public affairs director, Bryan Thomlison, says the system makes Church & Dwight "the only company in the world that can demonstrate with hard data a ten-to-one return on its public affairs budget... Any company that doesn't tie contributions to its core competencies to meet strategic business objectives is wasting money."

Another notable difference between "pure" philanthropy and strategic giving is in the density and diffusion of donations. The old "smorgasbord" approach of donating small sums to many disparate groups has given way to much more targeted grant-making. Strategic givers tend to pick one or two areas in which to make grants—typically areas with a direct impact on their community or on their business—and spend larger sums in those areas. Hence we see insurance companies targeting AIDS education and AIDS research, bookstores targeting illiteracy, food processing companies targeting food banks and soup kitchens.

> Daimler-Benz (now Daimler-Chrysler) has invested over $5 million in programs in the Amazon Rainforest in Brazil. The money supports a variety of programs to protect and improve the lives of the indigenous peoples of the area, as well as the environment. Why would a German car manufacturer care about the rainforest? Simple—they have plant operations in the area.

> The Gap Foundation's giving strategies look quite different now than they did when the Foundation started over twenty years ago. Originally, the Foundation gave small grants to a wide variety of causes. In 1990 the Foundation focused in two areas: helping elderly and youth programs in low-income communities, and helping the environment. In 1997 the program shifted focus again, this time on

Young People at Work (primarily thirteen- to twenty-five-year-olds and women) and AIDS. What brought about this latest change? The Foundation has grown, with a staff of more than ten and a budget of $8 million in cash and merchandise. According to Molly White, the Foundation's senior director, "It's time to start thinking about strategic investment." Young People at Work is a natural connection, with the majority of the Gap's 60,000 jobs entry level in nature. A majority of the Gap's customer base fits the bill. AIDS is a natural connection as well, being of major interest to a large number of Gap employees in San Francisco and New York.

"Pure" philanthropists often give grants anonymously or with little fanfare. At least, that's the generalization. In addition to the many anonymous donations, there were plenty of banquets and affairs where credit was given where it was due. When it comes to strategic giving, making the world a better place definitely is something to brag about. Since most gifts are designed to build goodwill, the more people who know, the better. In fact, a public relations campaign is often used to support the program.

> Until recently Midland Bank in the UK donated to approximately 250 charities each year. The guidelines the Bank used were often broad and undefined—the amounts often under £1,000. And the results, both in terms of public relations value to the company and impact to the charities, were often inconsequential. When Belinda Furneaux-Harris became head of sponsorship and donations for Midland, she began a review of the company's charitable giving. After a year, she decided to focus the bank's giving policies on three "charity partners." Shelter, a national campaign for the homeless, would receive £180,000 annually for three years. Age Concern, a charity that provides support services for the elderly, would receive £65,000 a year for the same period. And the National Deaf Children's Society would also garner £65,000 over the period. The three partners were picked on the basis of positive public relations opportunities and relevance to Midland's markets. Young people account for half the bank's new business, and issues of homelessness,

drug abuse, and unemployment had particularly high resonance with them. The elderly were a market in which Midland wanted to increase its representation. And the choice of a charity that works with the disabled not only appealed to customers that were disabled, but also coincided with the impending passage of the Disability Discrimination Act, bringing a high likelihood of public relations opportunity.

The Shape of Things to Come?

Will more companies adopt strategic giving in the future? Undoubtedly. With companies under increasing pressure to do more with less, the strategy is too effective to ignore. The Daniel Yankelovich Group, a New York market research firm, surveyed 225 chief executives of major corporations and one hundred executives described as "next generation CEOs" in a study for The Council on Foundations. Seventy-one percent felt that a company must determine the benefits to the business of each cause it supports. The next generation CEOs were particularly adamant about the need to emphasize corporate self-interest in giving policy. Another indication that the trend is here to stay is the number of specialty companies that have sprung up in the past three to four years just to support strategic giving. These companies consult with corporations, foundations, and individuals on methods for getting the maximum return from their charitable gifts. They help target social concerns that match business needs, and then build customized giving strategies.

Questions about Strategic Philanthropy

The rise of strategic philanthropy raises a lot of questions. For instance, is it really philanthropy, or is it really business-building disguised as a tax-deductible contribution? Are corporate philanthropists being co-opted by their colleagues in marketing and corporate communications? Are some nonprofits endangered by this trend? And, last but not least, is "pure" philanthropy dying? Let's take these questions one at a time.

1. *Is it really philanthropy?*
   Yes. Emphatically. (We can already hear grumbling.)
   On the most fundamental level, strategic giving is philanthropy

because the money comes from the corporate foundation and must meet IRS guidelines for its use. Alternately, money for business CRM ventures with nonprofits comes from the business side of the ledger.

On a more essential level, it's philanthropy because of its goal. A corporation's primary goal in strategic philanthropy is to use its money to make a difference in the world by benefiting a nonprofit. Its primary goal in a business venture is to benefit the corporation. This is a very important difference. Corporations give money to art museums because they know art museums need support. They fund programs in public schools because government funds are inadequate. That corporate benefits are tied to those goals does not diminish their philanthropic objectives.

If business benefits were the primary goal, corporations would be better off funding the programs with money from their business budgets. Those budgets are larger, they have fewer strings attached, and business expenses are just as tax-deductible as philanthropic expenditures. There is no advantage to using philanthropic dollars to fund business-building programs. In fact, most corporate foundations specifically prohibit it.

The Burger King Academies is an example of a strategic philanthropy. Many of Burger King's 250,000 employees are sixteen- to eighteen-year olds. In conjunction with their British parent company, GrandMetropolitan, Burger King has created thirty-one Burger King Academies in the U.S., and two in the United Kingdom. These efforts dovetail with relationships in both countries with Cities in Schools (CiS and CiS UK) to restore troubled youth into mainstream education and normal life. Youth employment and training programs like these may win customers and improve the skills of future employees, but there are less expensive ways of building business.

2. *Are corporate philanthropists being co-opted by marketers?*

Not the smart ones. Shrewd corporate givers get as much as they give when they work with colleagues in marketing. In exchange for involving the marketers in their philanthropic decisions, they snare marketing resources for their grant recipients. Instead of just writing a check to a nonprofit, they offer the agency a full-blown publicity campaign. This is manna from heaven to nonprofits, whose missions involve getting the word out to the public about what they are doing. Frequently, corporate givers tap other corporate resources as well. They work with human relations to recruit employee volunteers. They set up employee donation programs. They include information about the nonprofit in their customer mailings. In fact, for all these reasons, nonprofits are better served by strategic philanthropy than they are by simply receiving a check.

3. *Are nonprofits endangered by this trend?*

No. Nonprofits benefit from this trend. Strategic philanthropy isn't just strategic for the corporation. It is equally strategic for the nonprofit because it mobilizes a variety of corporate resources to carry out the agency's mission. It is the vehicle of choice for companies that seriously want to make a difference. And as we've shown earlier, strategic philanthropy is one of the major places picking up the slack in nonprofit funding left by decreased government support, lower relative personal contributions, and shrinking "pure" philanthropy.

4. *Is "pure" philanthropy dying?*

Even the most ardent practitioners of strategic philanthropy still engage in "pure" philanthropy as well. As long as United Way exists, as long as chief executives have a say, companies will still give money to worthy causes. The tradition of "pure" philanthropy is too ingrained in our culture to peter out, no matter how tight money gets.

In fact, most companies that practice strategic philanthropy do so with only a small number of their grant recipients, if only because working strategically with a partner takes more time and effort than writing a check. Staff people need to carefully select the partner, orchestrate an event or campaign, and work with the partner as they do it. It's a time-consuming process. So don't look for "pure" philanthropy to die out soon. Writing a check will always be the quickest and easiest way to benefit a nonprofit. It's just not necessarily the most effective way for the nonprofit, the corporation, or the community at large.

13

THERE ARE NO RULES!

"You can't have the biggest force in society, business, concerned only with maximizing profits and still have a socially responsible society."
— Ben Cohen, of Ben & Jerry's

<   <   <   <

Because strategic corporate citizenship is still evolving, each successful venture may launch an entirely new category. And some pretty creative, pretty innovative individuals are at the cutting edge of strategic corporate citizenship, looking "outside of the box" for their next innovation.

Take Listerine and Rosie O'Donnell. When Scope declared Rosie O'Donnell "unkissable," Warner-Lambert (the makers of Listerine) responded with an offer to donate $1,000 to Rosie's "For All Kids Foundation" for every on-air kiss between Rosie and her guests. By the time it was over, Listerine had received a market share increase (at Scope's expense), For All Kids Foundation had received $500,000 and Rosie's lips were ready to fall off. The promotion is now famous, but what was it? Calling it strategic philanthropy would be a stretch, and describing it as an in-kind donation isn't totally accurate, either, but where exactly should we put it in this book? In fact, if she keeps going, we'll need to give her a chapter of her own. Between sales of Rosie's book, *Kids Are Punny* and the talking Rosie O'Doll (a joint CRM venture between K Mart, Toys "R" Us, Tyco Preschool Toys, and Rosie), the For All Kids Foundation donated $1.5 million to 105 charitable organizations in its first fiscal year.

Which brings us to a man who invented his own special niche in the world of cause marketing, Paul Newman.

According to his own chronology (on his Web site), Paul Newman began making his own salad dressings in his basement in 1980. He officially launched the product at a press conference in August 1982 with a personal investment of $40,000 and no test-marketing. After an astounding first year profit of $920,000, Paul Newman said, "Let's give it all away to them what needs it."

Sixteen years later, in 1996, the total amount Paul Newman had donated through the sale of Newman's Own products topped $80 million.

Let's all just stop and think about that. In 1982, if anyone had said they could successfully run a company while donating 100 percent of after-tax profits to educational and charitable causes, they would have been laughed out of the room. The last thing we would have predicted is that less than two decades later the company would have a product line that included five salad dressings, six pasta sauces, a rather unique line of salsas, regular and microwave popcorn, lemonade, cookies, ice cream, and candy bars.

Or that more than 1,000 charities would benefit from his dream.

Today, Newman's Own Inc. all natural food products are available around the world. The company contracts to twelve manufacturers in the United States as well as licensees in England and Australia.

In addition, the company supports six Hole-in-the-Wall-Gang Camps, four in the United States and two abroad, for children suffering from cancer and other serious blood diseases. The first camp opened in 1988.

So why have we included this glowing advertisement for Mr. Newman? What does it tell you about cause-related marketing?

It tells you that you really can change the world. That business is an engine that can drive the biggest dreams to the highest heights. That you can break all the rules and still succeed beyond anyone's expectations.

The only thing stopping you from using your power is you.

In the next part of this book, we'll introduce you to the world of nonprofits. If you're going to work with them, you need to understand them. And believe us when we say they look at things differently than corporations do.

But before we do, we have one more thing we want to say.

$80 million dollars.

Thank you, Paul.

PART III

A NONPROFIT PRIMER

"We know we're successful when we leave a corporate meeting and they say, 'You know, you guys aren't like every other charity.' We're going to leave something on the table as well as take. You have to understand corporations. When they talk about marketing, you better be able to converse in that language."
—*Kurt Aschermann*
Senior VP Marketing
Boys & Girls Clubs of America

<   <   <   <

Working with a nonprofit is a little like going to a foreign country where the people speak English. At first everything looks pretty familiar. There are obvious differences, of course: cars drive on the "wrong" side of the road; they eat porridge instead of corn flakes; they wear "braces" where we wear suspenders. But you smile at those eccentricities—they're charming deviations in people who are otherwise kindred spirits. It's only as you stick around—read the papers, watch the "telly," get to know a "bloke" or two—that you realize the differences go deeper than you'd originally thought.

What's different, of course, is the culture—the values, the outlooks, the ways of approaching problems, the ways of relating to people—the millions of invisible things that make the country what it is. And of course precisely because they're invisible, those are the things that trip you up. You laugh at the wrong lines, you speak at the wrong moments, you move ahead when others wait and wait when others move ahead. Before long, you find yourself thinking, "It's so frustrating in this country! Why don't they do things the way we do?"

Eventually, if you're flexible, you realize the key to a successful visit is to learn a little of the culture and to stop expecting everything to be like home. Once you do that, you can appreciate the differences and get the most out of your visit.

Working with a nonprofit is similar. The outward differences—smaller offices, smaller budgets, smaller salaries—mask fundamental cultural differences underneath. Those differences are not impenetrable. In fact, they are quite negotiable. Some of them—like the nonprofit focus on mission—are the reason you've chosen to partner with a nonprofit in the first place. With a little patience and a little guidance, you should navigate quite smoothly. To help you, we offer a "traveler's guide" to the world of nonprofits.

Mission First, Money Second

The first thing that separates nonprofits from for-profits is a very different sense of mission. For corporations, "mission" means profit. Profits are the goal of the business. Ultimately, they drive most decisions.

For nonprofits, "mission" has a very different meaning. It has nothing to do with money and everything to do with saving the world. Whether it's educating children, supporting people with AIDS, saving baby seals, or performing a symphony, what drives nonprofit staffs, boards, and volunteers is the belief that by doing what they do, they make the world a better place.

That's not to say that nonprofit people are self-important. (If anything, their often precarious finances keep them humble.) Rather it's to say that most nonprofit people believe strongly in what they do. That's why they do it—certainly not for the money, which is less than they would make in the for-profit world. This belief in what they do colors all their thinking. It is the yardstick against which all decisions are measured. It becomes, in effect, their bottom line.

Money Matters

To say that nonprofits are mission-driven is not to say that they don't think about money. On the contrary, they think about money all the time. Mostly they think about where to get it. The chronic need to raise money—and the constraints on operations that need creates—are major shapers of nonprofit culture.

Take the YMCA. The need to find operating revenues has changed the nature of the YMCA, from an organization designed to promote the "spirit, mental, and social condition of young men" into a chain of middle-class family health and fitness centers. They are still serving the needs of the community, but not in the way they used to.

Even for large, entrepreneurial nonprofits, funding is a major concern. Money comes from various sources, most of them uncontrollable. Grants are subject to the whim of the funding agency—government, foundation, or corporation. Individual donations must be solicited each year. Memberships and program fees are relatively stable, but cover only a portion of expenses. As a result, lots of time and energy is spent considering where the next dollars come from. This is done primarily by the executive director, with help in medium to large nonprofits from the development director or development department. But even people at the low end of the organization feel the ebb and flow of budget worries as programs are added and cut with each year's changing income.

This chronic shortage of money has understandable repercussions on non-profit staffing. The most obvious is the unavoidable reliance on volunteers. This is generally not a matter of choice—paid staff are far easier to manage. But money being what it is, and necessity being the mother of invention, most nonprofits have become skillful volunteer managers. They've learned how to recruit desirable volunteers and train them, how to motivate them, how to evaluate them regularly and positively, and how to compensate them effectively with education, respect, meaningful work, and appreciation. They've accepted the fact that working with volunteers means things happen more slowly, require more patient explanation, and need more group buy-in than if the staff were all paid.

The second repercussion of chronically tight budgets is under-staffing. Almost all nonprofits are seriously understaffed, with most people working very long hours, often doing more than one job. Their loyalty to the institution and to the cause tends to keep them in their jobs, but staff burnout is a chronic problem. Nonprofits also tend to have many part-time staffers, in part to reduce costs by keeping salaries lower, and in part to accommodate women who want to spend time at home with their children.

Decision by Committee

Decisions in nonprofits require consensus. Committees—of the board, of staff, of volunteers—are involved, and actions may be belabored or postponed if an important person is unavailable. Be warned: at some point in your joint venture you'll need a fast decision and your partner will be unable to comply. This can be a sore point in joint ventures. Flexibility is needed on both sides.

How Nonprofits View Cause-Related Marketing

Most nonprofits will approach a corporate partnership with mixed feelings. On the one hand, they want the benefits the co-venture can offer. On the other, they are fearful of appearing too commercial, of appearing to have sold out to a corporation in exchange for cash. Don't misunderstand. This fear is not based on dislike for money or for business. It is based on a nonprofit's overwhelming concern for its integrity.

Nonprofit Integrity

Integrity is a nonprofit's most valuable possession. It is the thing the organization cherishes—and protects—above all else. This is vital to understand if you are going to work with a nonprofit, because there is nothing quite like it in the for-profit world, yet it will be at the heart of your negotiations.

A nonprofit's concern with its integrity is similar to, but different from, a company's concern about its image. You carefully cultivate your image, you try to protect it from bad press, you hope it represents you well to the world. But corporate images are created with advertising. If need be, they can be altered with a new campaign.

They are in some ways external to the company itself. A nonprofit's integrity, on the other hand, is its soul and essence. It is the reason people believe in the organization—and the reason people give it money. If a nonprofit's integrity is sullied, at worst, the organization's existence may be threatened. At best, heads—of the director, the board, the staff—will roll.

What exactly is nonprofit integrity? It is a combination of things. It is the nonprofit's image, the way it appears to the public. It is the organization's reputation for doing what it does well and honestly. It is what the organization represents: the hope that whatever problem it is tackling will be solved. But most important, it is the fact that the organization does what it does for public gain, not for the benefit of private individuals. Because of that, the public believes in the organization and trusts it. And that trust must not be betrayed. It is to preserve that trust that nonprofits guard their integrity so jealously.

Of course, that is precisely where nonprofits differ from corporations. Corporations do exist for private gain, and are not trusted by the public the same way. That's one of the reasons strategic alliances benefit you—and it's precisely what nonprofits fear. They fear that by working closely with you, they will appear to be doing what they are doing for money, rather than for the public good—that your offer of money will appear to sway them from their pure, altruistic mission and, as a result, make their programs less trustworthy.

Obviously, this fear doesn't stop many nonprofits from engaging in strategic partnerships. But it does create requirements that their partners must meet. Most nonprofits require that their partners' products and services be compatible with their mission (no cigarette companies for the Cancer Society) and that the campaign be designed to promote their mission by getting the word out to promote their cause. If you understand their needs in this regard, you'll find dealing with a nonprofit partner much easier.

Implied Endorsements

The way nonprofits guard their integrity is by being fiercely protective of their names and logos. How those items are used—where they appear and for how long—is of great concern, and rightly so. Nonprofits have everything to lose if a logo is used inappropriately. The greatest concern is that their name and logo will be used to imply endorsement of a company's product or service. Few nonprofits will agree to that. Nonprofits see it as the surest way to threaten the trust placed in them by their members, funders, and supporters.

Nonprofits generally try to avoid implied endorsements by avoiding joint ventures with companies that make products they don't want to endorse, or by asking that materials include the company name rather than a product name. Of course, your company may want the implied endorsement—that may be one of the reasons you sought the relationship. But as you negotiate your partnership terms, you'll need to be sensitive to your partner's concerns. It may help to remember that you've sought this partner because you want to associate with its integrity and image. It's in your interest to keep that image uncommercial.

The American Red Cross is an organization that has successfully linked its name to corporations. In 1995 the Red Cross allowed MCI to link its name with theirs, in return for MCI's contribution of some of its proceeds from long distance calls. For $1 million, the Red Cross lets companies tie their names to theirs through sponsored advertising. And the Red Cross licensed their logo to Sirena Swimwear for use on its swimsuits.

Implied Endorsements: Procter & Gamble and the Arthritis Foundation

Unfortunately, implied endorsements are just that—implications—and sometimes even the best intentions can't prevent them. Procter & Gamble found this out when it developed a joint venture with the Arthritis Foundation.

P&G had just developed a new plastic snap top for its king-size box of Tide. As an employee of the company played with the lid one day, he realized that it was very easy to open and close—that, in fact, this might be the only detergent box someone with arthritis could open and close without help.

The company approached the Arthritis Foundation to see whether it would be interested in a joint venture. The foundation agreed. Partnership with the giant consumer goods manufacturer would meet several of its needs. The organization was interested in achieving greater visibility with the public. With a public recognition factor of just two percent, it welcomed exposure for its name and logo. The foundation also welcomed the cash. So the two organizations agreed on a year-long arrangement in which the new Tide box would bear the nonprofit's logo and the words "commended by the Arthritis Foundation." In addition, P&G did two Sunday newspaper coupon promotions in which it offered a percentage of all Tide sales to the foundation. The foundation netted $200,000.

All seemed well until the company started getting phone calls from people who wanted to know how Tide could help their arthritis. The company had to explain that it was not the product that was commended, but merely the packaging. Despite the best efforts to make the "commendation" clear, it was still misunderstood by some customers. As someone at the foundation later said, "You know, perception is reality. As long as our logo was there, no matter what we said, some people were going to perceive what they wanted to believe."

What Nonprofits Want from a Joint Venture

Nonprofits want three things from strategic partnerships. You can think of them as the three M's: money, message, and members.

Money > The most valuable return by far from a campaign is money. It is made even more valuable by the fact that, in most campaigns, unless the corporation deems otherwise, the money is unrestricted. That is, the nonprofit can use it however it wants. This is different from most nonprofit income streams, which are earmarked for special projects. Whereas grants are usually given for a new ballet, a particular environmental campaign, a particular program for inner-city teens, or some other specially designated project, unrestricted cash can be used to pay the rent, the utility bill, even the staff.

Message > The mission is the message. That's why nonprofits exist. Whether it's teaching about tropical rainforests or working to end a disease, the nonprofit's mission means getting a message out to the public. And that's exactly what campaigns are designed to do. With all the marketing resources of a corporation behind it, a nonprofit can reach many more people than it would ever reach on its own.

Members > To keep themselves going, nonprofits depend on individual members. These people are the lifeblood of the organization: they pay dues, they volunteer, they write their members of Congress, they support the organization's work so that it can advance its goals. By reaching thousands or even millions of people with the nonprofit's message, a campaign can win new members for the organization.

What They Will Ask

Nonprofits will have several concerns going into a joint venture. These are the kinds of questions they will ask themselves—and you—as they consider doing a campaign.

Mission-Related > Does this venture help us in our mission? (If the answer is no, most nonprofits will choose not to participate for fear the venture will jeopardize their IRS tax-exempt status, offend supporters, and divert them from their regular responsibilities.)

Corporate Reputation > Is this corporation one with which we want to be associated? Do we approve of their products or services? Are they the subject of any controversy? Are they socially responsible? Are they a suitable image match for us? Will we lose funding from others by partnering with them?

Implied Endorsements > Can we partner this company without appearing to endorse its products? How can the campaign be designed accordingly?

Existing Relationships > Will entering this venture jeopardize our relationships with other funders—other corporations, foundations, major donors, our members?

Negative Press Potential > Can this joint venture reflect badly on us in any way?

Commercialization vs. Credibility > Will we lose our credibility by doing this? Will we appear to be selling out by selling our name?

Responsibilities > What will our responsibilities be? How much time will this take from our regular duties?

Money > How much money are we likely to make? What's the minimum? Maximum? Are there any guarantees? Will we have any costs?

Control > Will we have control over how our name and logo are used? Will we be able to review all campaign material?

Audience > Who will this campaign reach? Are those our target audiences?

How One Nonprofit Does It: The American Cancer Society

For years, the American Cancer Society (ACS) eschewed corporate partnerships because of concern about implied endorsements. But, recently, ACS changed its mind. ACS believes that co-ventures hold too many opportunities for raising money and for promoting its message to pass them up. So with a new corporate relations staff person heading the effort, the Society is now exploring avenues for cause-related marketing and formulating policies that will help it protect its integrity. It is looking carefully at how it can select partners, structure the ventures, and avoid the problem of implied endorsements.

Picking Partners

ACS is regularly approached by companies that want to create joint ventures. The Society turns down 95 percent of these requests because the company or the proposed joint venture is unsuitable. To be considered for a venture, a company must meet two requirements:

> The company and its products must be compatible with the Society's mission. ACS will not partner a company that produces unhealthy food, tobacco or alcohol products, or any product that counters its mission of promoting a healthy lifestyle.

> The company must be well established. ACS wants to know its partners can deliver the goods. The Society also believes that its partners' images reflect on them. So it chooses companies whose stature and image are on a par with its own.

Structuring the Relationship

Many of the requests ACS receives are rejected because they are exploitative. They come from companies that want to use the ACS name to sell their product, but offer little in return. Or they want to sell to the ACS donor list, a practice the Society prohibits. Or they propose returns that are too small for the effort required: for example, a year-long nationwide promotion netting the Society only $5,000 to $10,000. For ACS to agree to a co-venture, the campaign must provide a significant amount of money, and it must genuinely promote the Society's message and mission.

For instance, when ACS planned a two-year joint venture with Doncaster, a women's clothing manufacturer, it had to meet both of these requirements. Rather than selling retail, Doncaster distributes its clothing through a network of "fashion consultants," women who sell the clothing out of their homes. Four times a year, the company sends consultants new wardrobes. The consultants then schedule private showings with friends and associates. In the ACS venture, Doncaster would buy educational material from the Society about cancers common to women. The company would distribute the material to its fashion consultants, who would then discuss it with their clients. In addition, Doncaster would donate to the Society one dollar from every sale. In this way, the Society would net a significant financial return, a projected $400,000 to $500,000. It would also have its message promoted in a very direct way.

Avoiding Implied Endorsements

The Doncaster partnership is also exemplary in that it completely avoids the problem of implied endorsements. Since there are no links between clothing and cancer, there is no implication that ACS endorses Doncaster clothes as good for preventing the disease.

But the Society realizes that CRM opportunities will arise with companies whose products are not so clearly removed from cancer. Food companies, for instance, would make natural partners, especially as food manufacturers continue to make health claims for their products. Would ACS agree to partner a company that makes vitamin supplements? Probably not—because although the Society doesn't disapprove of vitamin supplements, it prefers to stress the importance of eating a balanced diet. What about a cereal manufacturer? Possibly—if the cereal was healthful and if the Society could adequately explain its position to the public.

In any campaign with the potential for an implied endorsement, the Society insists on explaining its position. It will require that the relationship between the Society and the company be clearly spelled out in campaign material. For example, "X company will donate Y cents to ACS for every coupon redeemed." And in some campaigns the Society may insist on a disclaimer, stating that ACS does not endorse the product. But ACS also realizes that ultimately it can't control what consumers think. Occasionally, despite careful choices and disclaimers, some consumers may take the ACS name on a commercial label as an endorsement of that product. The Society won't be happy, but is willing to take the risk in order to reap the benefits of strategic partnership.

The Ten Commandments of Strategic Alliances: A Nonprofit's View

To reassure you that there are nonprofits out there who understand business and how to work with you, we've reprinted Kurt Aschermann's "Ten Commandments of Cause-Related Marketing" (we've replaced *CRM* with our more inclusive term, *strategic alliance*). Aschermann is the vice president of marketing for Boys & Girls Clubs of America, a nonprofit that's done an amazing job of transforming itself into a joint venture machine. (We'll tell you more about them in chapter 15.) Remember, this is how smart nonprofits see themselves. If you understand these rules, you will have a better chance to forge a real partnership when they're sitting across the table from you.

1. **Understand Your Product.** You have to know the value your organization brings to the relationship. Communicate this proposition clearly and concisely, and be prepared to stick to your guns if a potential partner doesn't agree. "B&GCA was recently approached by two different companies who thought that we would be thrilled to work with them. Neither firm thought that we, a nonprofit, brought much to the table. They thought we'd want to work with them because of who they were. We politely turned them down. The truth is, we bring enormous value to a corporate partner. We have to understand and articulate this value."

2. **Understand Business and How It Works.** You don't need an MBA, but when a partner talks about "market share" you need to understand the jargon.

3. **Follow Classic Account Management Principles.** Classic account management means that one person handles a B&GCA partner's account, and acts as that partner's principle contact within the organization.

4. **Each Partner Must Believe that They Are Your Only Partner.** Each B&GCA project—such as Coke, Bonnie Raitt/Fender Music, Mervyn's, or Finish Line—has its own "account manager," as well as a backup person. When a partner calls, they get an answer. Even if their primary contact is out, the call is referred to another team member.

5. **Leave the Paper at Home.** Some of B&GCA's best proposals happen without paper. Bringing in a written proposal, an actual document, to the first meeting gives the potential partner the option of saying no. B&GCA practices "proposal-less fundraising," listening to the partner, identifying its needs, and then crafting a proposal with the partner. This gives them a sense of ownership in the project. At the same time, make sure the potential partner knows what B&GCA is all about.

6. **Patience Is a Virtue.** Joint ventures take time. It took a year before the Coca-Cola partnership came to fruition. Major League Baseball took four years.

7. **Listen Up.** Listening is a lost art. Everyone wants to talk, to get their point across. B&GCA learns a lot about potential partners just by listening.

8. **Strategic Alliances Are a Team Effort.** Five staff members and five B&GCA governors direct strategic alliance efforts.

9. **Strategic Alliances Are an Agency-Wide Effort.** Everyone thinks about fundraising at B&GCA.

10. **Strategic Alliances Are About Relationships.** All these "commandments" are nothing more than examples of good relationship management. People give money to people. People do more for those they like and trust, and who care. Strategic alliances are about caring for your partner's needs.

Now, which way to the promised land?

15

ENTREPRENEURIAL NONPROFITS

"Our nonprofit organizations are becoming America's management leaders... They are practicing what American businesses only preach... working out the policies and practices that business will have to learn tomorrow."
— Peter F. Drucker

< < < <

Nonprofits practicing what businesses only preach? Using today what business will learn tomorrow? Not exactly the standard thinking on nonprofits. But Peter Drucker has made his name by espousing new ways of thinking. Maybe it's time to take another look at the nonprofit sector?

The last two decades have brought huge changes to the ways nonprofits think and act. While corporations experienced their own spurts of growth and recession, nonprofits endured parallel turmoil. With nonprofit fortunes closely tied to the health of business and government, these organizations thrived in the early 1980s, but lost much of their traditional funding since then. Some were forced to close. Others scaled back their programs. But many nonprofits used the opportunity to go back to the drawing board and rethink the ways they operate. These organizations emerged from the decade leaner and meaner, with new, businesslike attitudes in place and new management practices on board. These newly entrepreneurial nonprofits are well positioned for success—and they will make powerful business partners for the corporations smart enough to seize the opportunity to work with them.

One of the strongest examples of this entrepreneurial renaissance of nonprofits is Boys & Girls Clubs of America. You remember Boys & Girls Clubs of America, don't you? The old "swim and gym" clubs in your home town? The first club opened in 1860, and the national organization first took shape in 1906 (although it wasn't called the B&GCA yet.) As the B&GCA entered the 1990s, the club was faced with a dilemma. Even their staunchest corporate supporters began asking club executives, "Is there some value in this for my business?"

Rather than fade away, the B&GCA decided to fight for their survival. They reorganized their board into "one of the most influential boards in the country" according to Kurt Aschermann, senior VP marketing for B&GCA. "We have a board full of capitalists," says Aschermann. "Their perspective is simple: Find and fill a need." The board includes General Colin Powell, John Antioco of Blockbuster, Roberto Goizveta of Coca-Cola, Don Fischer, founder of The Gap, Liz Dolan, head of marketing at Nike, Rick Goings of Tupperware, Harvey Schiller, president of Turner Sports, and actor Denzel Washington, an alumnus of the B&GCA.

After the reorganization, B&GCA chairman Rick Goings invested in a joint marketing strategy. The goals: to establish relationships with the largest name brand, a sports league, and a major network. They brought in marketing professionals who "began asking corporations what it was they wanted from us, and told them what we were doing," says Aschermann.

The strategy paid off. Here are some of their recent corporate partnerships:

> Coca-Cola: $60 million over ten years.

> Major League Baseball: $1.5 million over five years.

> The TBS SuperChallenge: The goal is one million hours of volunteer time, matched by TBS with $1 million for the national organization and $1 million for the local clubs.

> Taco Bell: $15 million over five years.

> Swatch/Goodwill Games: A portion of the proceeds of a special Goodwill Games watch, proceeds estimated between $7-10 million.

> Partners include the All-State Foundation, Blimpie, Brink's Home Security, Computer City, Enesco, Bonnie Raitt/Fender Music,

Finish Line, Old Navy Clothing Co., *Reader's Digest, Sports Illustrated*, Starbuck's, and Uptons.

What's in it for these companies? The B&GCA numbers are pretty impressive: 2,800,000 boys and girls, at 866 local organizations and 2,065 Club facilities, in all fifty states, Puerto Rico, the Virgin Islands plus domestic and international military bases. In addition to all that, the club staff itself: 8,000 trained youth workers, 20,000 part-time staffers and 95,500 volunteers.

According to Aschermann, "Our success is because our partners are partners, not just funding sources." And success it is. In its latest "Philanthropy 400" report, the *Chronicle of Philanthropy* ranked the B&GCA as the number one youth organization (for the fourth consecutive year) and ninth among all nonprofits. The survey, which measures private support, reported gifts totaling $437 million in 1996.

>   >   >   >

In the first part of this book, we looked at the challenges facing business in the 1990s and beyond. Now let's take a look at the challenges that faced nonprofits over the past few years—and the ways entrepreneurial nonprofits have responded.

Challenge #1: Government Cutbacks

Most nonprofits get the lion's share of their operating income from federal, state, and local governments. Governments mandate the provision of social services and pay nonprofits to deliver them. Since the 1980s, government cutbacks have played havoc with this relatively dependable source of income. Over the decade, federal government grants decreased by 20 percent and nonprofit groups lost $30 billion in direct aid. Budget shortfalls at the state and local levels compounded the crisis.

As we pointed out earlier, the budget resolution passed by Congress in 1996 called for a cumulative reduction of 18 percent of federal support for nonprofits from 1997-2002. This works out to $90 billion of lost government funding to hospitals, colleges, universities, social service agencies, civic organizations, and the arts. And we're not even addressing changes in the way the government taxes nonprofits, which can result in even larger operating deficits.

Governments are also replacing grants to nonprofit agencies with fee-for-service contracts. This saves money for the government, but presents a problem for nonprofits. Grants provide funds for general operating overhead. Fee-for-service contracts don't. As a result, nonprofits have lost much of the unrestricted money that kept the rent paid, the lights on, and their other programs operating. Unfortunately, cutbacks in government funding have come just when the need for service is increasing. AIDS, illiteracy, homelessness, substance abuse, child abuse, poverty, and numerous other problems are at an all-time high and are expected to increase.

The Entrepreneurial Nonprofit Response

Entrepreneurial nonprofits have seen the writing on the wall. Recognizing that government funds are unlikely to increase any time soon, they have developed revenue-producing lines of business to replace lost income. These ventures are designed to provide stable, continuing revenue. For example:

> In 1994-95, government funding for the Parks Canada program was cut by 6.9 percent, with a further 6.2 percent cut for 1995-96. Combined with increased visitation to the parks and increased competition for private funding (against, among others, the WWF), these cuts seriously threatened the preservation and protection of Canadian parks. The nonprofit Canadian Parks Partnership (CPP) responded with a three-way initiative involving the government, private industry, and themselves. Parks Canada granted CPP the right to use their logo and enter into partnerships with corporations such as Hi-Tech Sports (Canada) Ltd., Kodak Canada, Duracell Canada, General Motors of Canada, Hallmark, Post Cereal, and others. The first two years of these efforts generated revenues for the Canadian Parks Partnership in excess of $700,000 and got the message out to seven million Canadians. In one of the co-ventures, Hi-Tech sports developed a line of "Canada Parks" apparel and hiking boots. CPP's message reached 500,000 Canadians via hang tags on the products, and more than 300,000 TV viewers saw the national ads each week. As a result of the program, the CPP achieved financial self-sufficiency, and enabled them to expand their services, and even estab-

lish a Parks fund to support education, research, and restoration projects in national parks and historic sites.

Challenge #2: The Slowdown in Corporate and Private Giving

Business is another big benefactor of nonprofit organizations, but corporate contributions haven't risen at the pace of the cost of living.

> The spate of mergers and acquisitions has reduced the number of givers.

> Many companies that survived restructuring are saddled with debt.

> Several large corporations with long traditions of corporate giving have been bought by foreign owners who don't share that tradition.

> Many companies are offering corporate volunteers and in-kind contributions in lieu of cash.

> The new entrepreneurial elite and super rich have been slow to join the front ranks of private donorship (although Bill Gates's $3.34 billion donation in 1999 is a heck of a start).

As money gets tighter, businesses are holding nonprofits increasingly accountable for the money they receive. They are evaluating nonprofits' fiscal health and management before making grants to make sure their investments will be well spent. They are favoring one-time-only grants, encouraging nonprofit recipients to become self-sufficient. They are offering matching grants, requiring nonprofits to augment their dollars with funds from other sources. And they are evaluating funded programs for effectiveness. This trend has added to the fundraising pressures already felt by nonprofits. While the demands are reasonable, they mean more hoops to jump through to raise the necessary cash.

The Entrepreneurial Nonprofit Response

Entrepreneurial nonprofits have begun to decrease their dependence on fundraising and develop new ways to earn money. Strategies range from the sale of products and services related to the agencies' missions to the development of freestanding, for-profit businesses whose revenues subsidize the organization. For example:

> In November of 1994, the British government launched the National Lottery. Some of the proceeds of the lottery were earmarked for charity, with the result that by September 1995 charitable contributions had fallen off £61 million, according to the National Council for Voluntary Organisations. Three of the hardest hit charities were Age Concern, the British Heart Foundation, and the Cancer Research Fund. To replace their lost funding, the three, along with Help the Aged, co-founded Charity Flowers Direct, a for-profit concern that sells fresh flowers by mail. For their investment, each of the founders will receive a share of the trading profits. Plus, 20 percent of the purchase price of the bouquets will go to one of the four charities, to be determined by the purchaser. The company estimates that the charities will split £1 million each year. According to the business development director of Age Concern, "We have created an environment where major charities can work together as shareholders in a 'mint fundraising venture.'" He's certainly gotten other charities in the United Kingdom excited: forty of them have asked to join.

Challenge #3: The Rise of Strategic Philanthropy

The rise of strategic philanthropy, as discussed in chapter 12, has caused considerable hand-wringing among nonprofits. Many fear the bottom-line approach will jeopardize their ability to raise money through philanthropic donations. Some of the most concerned are purely humanitarian groups that don't bring appeal to a large special interest group.

The Entrepreneurial Nonprofit Response

While others debate its merits, entrepreneurial nonprofits have adopted a marketing partnership approach. Recognizing the commercial value of their names and services, they now ask companies with shared interests for a marketing partnership, rather than a donation to a worthy cause. For example:

> GuateSalud is an HMO serving the rural working poor in Guatemala. When it became difficult to raise funds through donations, the founders began selling their services to local coffee plantations. The workers at these plantations were mostly poor migrant workers hired only during harvests—the same people GuateSalud was trying to help in the first place. The plantation owners pay a monthly fee and the workers pay small fees for visits and prescriptions. The plantation owners get a healthier, and more productive workforce; the poor get better medical care than normally available to them; and GuateSalud gets to be more self-sufficient.

Challenge #4: Increased Competition for Individual Donors

Individual contributions to nonprofits are growing. Unfortunately, so is the number of nonprofits (at a rate of 30,000 per year). As a result, competition for individual donors is at an all-time high. For many nonprofits, this means a need to buckle down and do more of the same: buy more mailing lists, send more form letters, make more cold calls… and cross their fingers that enough people will respond.

The Entrepreneurial Nonprofit Response

Entrepreneurial nonprofits are trying something new—marketing. They are wooing new donors the same way business woos clients: by targeting selected groups and developing strategies aimed specifically at them. Among other things, they are developing marketing partnerships with corporations to win the attention of their customers—doing market research to locate their best donors and learn how to appeal to them effectively, and developing special events designed to attract potential donors.

> The eighty-five-year-old National Urban League has been credited with continually reinventing itself to keep up with the times and remain relevant. After becoming president in the mid 1990s, Hugh Price and his VP of development, Phyllis Buford, visited sixty corporations in twenty-five cities to drum up corporate support. Among the projects they pushed was the Urban League's "Youth Development Campaign," to provide social and educational pro-

grams to inner-city African American youth. The trip yielded a $1 million donation from Monsanto, $500,000 from Borden and a $50,000 grant from Citicorp.

Challenge #5: Increasing Expenses

For nonprofits as for business, money is shrinking and expenses are expanding. (The biggest and fastest-growing expense is employee health care.) Since most nonprofits don't offer products or services with built-in profit, increasing fees won't solve the problem. They can cut costs, but since nonprofit shops are already lean, cutting costs generally means cutting programs.

The Entrepreneurial Nonprofit Response

Entrepreneurial nonprofits have responded to the challenge by developing revenue producing ventures with built-in profits. The profits help pay for overhead and add a cushion against inflation. For example:

> The Gathering Place is a women's and children's shelter in central Denver that was endangered by shrinking federal funding and private donations. They already had a program in place where women in the shelter painted cards, which were sold by the shelter for one dollar. The women received seventy-five cents for each card sold. In an attempt to find alternate funds to keep the shelter open, the Gathering Place approached Current, a Colorado Springs-based card company, about selling their cards. Current now manufactures, packages, and markets three designs of the shelter's cards. It treats The Gathering Place like any other vendor, which has helped the shelter. "They have been an incredible company to work with because they keep us honest about this being a business," says Bebe Kleinman, the shelter's then director of development. "I'll say, 'Thank you for the donation,' and they say, 'This isn't a donation, it's a royalty.'" More important than the self-esteem, though, is the money. In the first month the cards were on sale in Current's catalog, more than 10,000 boxes were sold. The Gathering Place hopes to earn up to 20 percent of its annual budget from CRM ventures like this.

Challenge #6: Competition from Business

Business is slowly moving into the realm of social services. Child care, health care, education, substance abuse, elder care, recreation, and other areas that have traditionally been the domain of nonprofits are now becoming lucrative fields for business. For instance, almost all of the growth in hospital care and home health care from 1977 to 1992 has been grabbed by for-profit companies. In some areas corporations are contracting with government to provide services. In others they are developing businesses to meet the growing needs. As a result, nonprofits must now compete with business for both government contracts and clients. This puts additional strain on organizations already subject to numerous external pressures.

The Entrepreneurial Nonprofit Response

Entrepreneurial nonprofits have risen to the challenge in a variety of ways. They have become more businesslike—strengthening management, redesigning pricing and financial systems, implementing marketing techniques—in order to meet the competition head-on. They've become more sophisticated. They even have their own version of lobbying groups. The N.I.S.H. advocates that business source a percentage of their manufacturing and purchasing to the more than 2,000 nonprofits that can provide it. Many of those nonprofits employ people with disabilities, such as Goodwill Industries and Pioneer Human Services. Entrepreneurial nonprofits have even developed business partnerships with for-profits in order to offer services jointly. For example:

> Can you take people society has written off and profit from giving them a second chance? Yes, according to former Pioneer CEO Gary Mulhair, who termed what they do "operational philanthropy." "We're going to hire people you wouldn't. But in a year or so, you will—because they'll be citizens." Seattle's Pioneer Human Services began as a nonprofit shelter workshop in 1962. Currently, it integrates "jobs, housing, training, and support services to give people a sense of dignity and confidence and a better chance of successfully rejoining the community." It was founded by Jack Dalton, a recovering alcoholic and convicted felon. The former CEO, Gary Mulhair, is

a social entrepreneur who attended the University of Washington Graduate School of Business. Pioneer Industries, the organization's largest operation, has projected 1998 revenues of $45 million. Its the first nonprofit in the nation to win ISO 9002 certification, a benchmark for quality in the private sector. It employs more than 700 people, over 75 percent having suffered from drug or alcohol problems or served time in state or federal prisons. Clients include Boeing, Heart Interface, Leviton, Quinton Instruments, and Taco del Mar, and the list is growing rapidly. In 1997 the Ford Foundation announced that it would invest nearly $2.5 million in Pioneer. In January 1998 Pioneer used some of that money to buy Greater Seattle Printing & Mailing, a $6.5 million-a-year business. Says Mulhair, "We're good at this."

The Changing Face of Nonprofits

Given the tenor of the times, many nonprofits would have found these entrepreneurial behaviors on their own. But as it happens, they've had help. Renegades from the private sector—people who lost their jobs to restructurings or wanted more meaningful work than business offered—have shifted over to the nonprofit side. These new executives run their agencies the way they used to run their businesses—with the expectation that they will show a surplus at the end of the year. The only difference is that here, instead of paying the surplus out to stockholders, they plow it back into programs to help the agencies better meet their missions.

To help them run their shops, they are hiring MBAs and installing them as marketing directors and financial officers. They are sending veteran staffers to business seminars at Harvard and the Wharton School. They are bringing in business consultants to help them tackle specific problems.

There are clashes, to be sure. The nonprofit culture is still quite different from the corporate world. Decisions require consensus. More people—volunteers, staff members, board members—must be involved. All decisions must be weighed against the mission, regardless of economic benefit.

But within the mission-driven structure things are changing. The old nonprofit "virginity" is gone, replaced with a lust for enterprise. Blatant distrust of business has been replaced with the knowledge that business strategies can meet nonprofit goals. Gradually, these new nonprofits are carving a territory in which the merger of mission and market form a powerful team. A perfect example of this new spirit is TEDI in Washington, D.C.:

> Melissa Bradley isn't the kind of high-powered entrepreneur you expect to read about in *Inc.* or *Fortune.* She grew up poor, in a single parent household in a low income neighborhood in New Jersey. After graduating Georgetown University (later earning an MBA), she started Bradley Consulting at the age of 23 with $250 in personal savings and loans from friends and family. The company, which provided financial guidance to families with students in college and outplacement services to corporations, was worth over a million dollars when she sold it three years later. She took the money from the sale and used it to launch The Entrepreneurial Development Institute (TEDI). The Washington, D.C.-based nonprofit teaches low-income African American youth how to become entrepreneurs. TEDI recruits in public schools, housing projects, community centers and even adjudication centers. In five years the organization has reached 15,000 young people in twenty-six cities and three countries. Some of her kids' projects: several teenage mothers in Arlington, Virginia, produce and market bilingual coloring books, a group of adjudicated youth started a t-shirt company, a service that buys and delivers groceries for the elderly, neighborhood-based manicure and beauty services, and even Web site design. Says Bradley, "If I could do it, I figured they could too."

16

HOW TO WORK WITH A NONPROFIT PARTNER

"We consider ourselves partners with every nonprofit organization we support... 'Strategic' isn't the word for what we do; 'complimentary' is."

—Akiko Mitsui
Community Reinvestment Act (CRA) Officer
Fuji Bank & Trust Company

<   <   <   <

Ever notice how many problems occur simply because people are talking at each other instead of to each other? Having practiced now for several thousand years, you'd think we'd be better able to communicate. As anyone who's ever been a parent, a spouse, a teacher, or a businessperson can tell you, the majority of problems in any relationship occur because of poor communication.

Strategic alliances are no different. When problems crop up between the partners, it's almost always because people aren't talking clearly or listening attentively. For example: one partner expects the other to do something by a certain time. The partner with the obligation is running late. But instead of warning the other party that there's going to be a problem, on the appointed day the partner just doesn't deliver. Who wouldn't get upset?

Here's another example: the partners agree that their special event will be jointly staffed by company employees and nonprofit volunteers. However, they fail to specify how many staffers each side will provide. On the day of the event, thirty volunteers show up, but only five employees. The nonprofit volunteers are swamped—and furious. Who's at fault? If each side had specified numbers ahead of time, they could have recruited the needed number and avoided the problem.

Here's one more: in the joy of partnership, the partners fail to consider how their program will be presented to the press. During an interview, the non-profit's public relations person neglects to name each corporate division participating in the program. The division managers are angry. Of course, the problem wouldn't have occurred had they talked the issue through ahead of time.

All these problems occurred because of poor communication. The partners had different expectations. Reality disappointed them, and tensions arose.

These are not merely hypothetical cases. These are the types of problems most likely to waylay a campaign and precisely the procedural issues that bog down a joint venture. Fortunately, there's a relatively easy cure:

> Think through every aspect of your campaign before it begins.

> Define roles and responsibilities clearly at the outset.

> Build in checkpoints to make sure both partners' needs are being met.

If you do those things you can avoid surprises. And in joint ventures, as in financial statements, surprise is rarely a good thing.

Managing the Relationship

There are a few other things you can do to keep your relationship running smoothly. Most co-ventures have problems in the same places—the places where corporate and nonprofit cultures clash. Anticipating those frictions—and planning ahead—can minimize tensions. Here are some specific recommendations for keeping the relationship running well.

Timelines

The majority of problems concern timelines. Campaigns tend to be driven by marketplace needs and often require fast decisions, which, unfortunately, are not a nonprofit's strength.

You can anticipate the culture of the nonprofit, including those factors that tend to slow down decision-making—reliance on volunteers, part-time staff, the need for consensus. Anticipating the problem won't make it go away, but may make it easier to deal with.

The nonprofit can keep the number of people involved in decisions to a minimum by appointing a committee (rather than the whole board) to decide on policy issues and by using a small committee of key players to make campaign operating decisions. The nonprofit can also assign people with a marketing or business background to work on the campaign.

Additionally, as you work together planning your campaign:

> Create realistic (rather than optimistic) time frames for the project.

> Give the schedule more breathing room than if you were working alone.

> Clearly pin down all delivery, review, and sign-off dates ahead of time.

Spelling Out Roles and Responsibilities

Spelling out both parties' roles and responsibilities at the outset will prevent misunderstandings later. It will enable you to develop the program so both sides get what they want. It will help you understand how the other side thinks. You'll need to walk through every aspect of the campaign, considering everything that might happen—desirable and undesirable, expected and unexpected.

Here are some things to think through and spell out in writing:

Goals > What does each partner want to get out of the campaign? Be as specific as possible in terms of exposure, money, press, sales gains, etc. Are your goals compatible, or do they point up potential areas of conflict?

Permissions, Reviews, Vetoes > Spell out who can review what and when, and who can veto what and when. When can you use the nonprofit's name and logo? When can the nonprofit use yours? Are all elements of the program to be jointly reviewed?

Exclusivity > Is this relationship exclusive? If so, for how long? When will it end? If not, what other types of corporations or nonprofits can become involved with one or both partners? Can either partner review and veto a new prospective partner?

Promotion > How will the campaign be promoted? In what media? To what target audiences? Are certain promotions off limits? Who decides?

Money > How will money be raised? How much money do you expect the campaign to make? How will it be managed? How will it be distributed, and when? Will minimum and maximum amounts go to the nonprofit? Are there guarantees? What auditing procedures will be used?

Ownership > Who will own the campaign material? The ideas? The copyrights? If you plan a continuing relationship, do you need a licensing agreement?

Reporting > What reports will you generate at the end—money raised, sales figures, market research results? Who will see the reports? Who will pay for them? How will you report the results to the public?

Termination > When do you want the relationship to end? What might make it end sooner? Later? How will you deal with those eventualities?

Roles and Responsibilities > Who will do what in each organization? Will you use the nonprofit's staff? Its local chapters? Its volunteers? How many? For what tasks? What role will your employees play? Your sales force? Your franchisees? Your retailers? Who will coordinate the campaign elements? How much time will this take? What if you need to hire additional people: who will pay?

Obviously, this list is not exhaustive, nor can you know every answer before the campaign begins. But thinking through and discussing these questions will help both partners clarify and articulate their expectations. They will point up areas of potential conflict so that they can be resolved before the campaign begins rather than during its implementation.

Using Consultants

Some companies that develop campaigns use consultants to do so. Most often this happens when a consultant brings an idea for a campaign to a corporation and the corporation decides to participate. The consultants are generally from special-events planners, marketing firms, or public relations firms. Sometimes the consultants start off with the nonprofits, and try to shop their client's participation around to find the money.

Are consultants a good idea? It depends on your organization. A clear advantage of using a consultant is prior experience. If the consultant has managed joint ventures in the past, he or she can remove some of the headaches for you. The consultant can help you find an appropriate partner, and then play buffer between you. He or she can develop and critique ideas with relative objectivity, and can manage the details of the event, sparing both your staff and that of the nonprofit.

How much are those benefits worth? The answer, again, depends on the corporation. They are probably worth more to a company trying a joint venture for the first time than to one that's experienced. Experienced organizations are often better off on their own, since they'll have learned how to work with a nonprofit and how to tailor a campaign to their own needs.

PART IV

HOW TO ENGAGE IN SUCCESSFUL
STRATEGIC ALLIANCES

17

GETTING DOWN TO IT

"To see the right and not do it is cowardice."

—*Confucius*

< < < <

We've shown you how other companies have made money while making a difference. Now it's your turn. In this chapter, we'll help you set up your team, after we lay down a few of the ground rules you should consider at the start.

Commitment to the Game

Don't even think about entering into a joint venture if management doesn't support the idea. It takes too much time, too much effort, too much rewriting of rules. It won't fly unless upper management has given its full support. And the support has to be genuine. If the staff gets involved in a project like this because they think it's one of the boss's pet projects, the results could be just as unsatisfying.

Take the Long View

Preferably, that commitment should be long-term—longer than just one program. After all, your first program may not work. Or it may work, but not as well as you had hoped. You're learning. You're building new behaviors, new ways of working across departments, new ways of evaluating what you do. You need to move from thinking tactically to thinking strategically. You're building long-term goodwill. You're forging a long-term relationship with customers. You're achieving long-term social gains. You need to support that with a long-term strategy.

Give It Adequate Resources

Management needs to commit not only time to the program, but also resources. For example, a joint venture may draw on people from many departments. A joint venture demands start-up capital, probably from several different budgets. A joint venture frequently requires additional cash once it's underway. Management must be committed to providing all those resources. Management's role is to remain above the fray, to think for the long term, to stand behind the program so that it gets what it needs.

Give It Room to Maneuver

Strategic alliances involve breaking rules. Marketing and Human Resources don't usually work together? Guess what? In strategic alliances they do. Your corporate giving programs aren't evaluated for a bottom-line return? They are now. In a strategic alliance, making a difference without making money is called a "negative learning experience." Your corporate communications programs must absolutely, positively live within their budgets? Not any more. Strategic alliance programs often need more leeway.

In strategic alliances you're doing things your company has never done before. You're learning on the fly. You're making up the rules as you go along. Your program needs the freedom to do that. It needs permission to make mistakes. It needs permission to miss a deadline. It needs permission to borrow staff and money from other departments.

Your effort should be treated like an enterprise unit within the larger organization: free from some of the usual operating constraints, coddled a little so that it has room to grow, and free to borrow resources when it becomes necessary. Management must give it this room to maneuver so it has the room to succeed.

Get the Right People

Strategic alliances, like public service, have a tendency to bring out people who think that the will to make a difference is enough. Some people see these partnerships as an opportunity to do jobs they weren't qualified to do, but have always wanted to try. Often they're allowed to do it by fellow employees who wanted to "give them a chance." Account executives who always wanted to write ads get to write them—badly. Art directors who wanted to try their hand at management will manage—ineffectively. This is like some non-profit organizations in the good old days: well-meaning do-gooders with the desire to help, but no skill set. They figured since they were volunteering, they weren't under pressure to perform. Executives took a back seat to avoid appearing bossy, employees wouldn't criticize or help for fear of being rude.

We mention this because we've spent decades struggling to turn nonprofits into effective, efficient organizations. Enthusiasm is nice, but effectiveness and profitability are critical. If you don't give it a chance to succeed, it won't. Use professionals in the areas that require experience or skill, let employees help the pros or work in jobs they can handle. When you do this, you empower them, allowing them to step outside of themselves by giving them the chance to succeed, not to become frustrated by jobs they bit off but couldn't swallow.

Don't ever forget why you're here: to make money while doing good. There are no points for doing good but losing money. Leave that to the charities and the politicians.

Building the Team
Team Captain/Enterprise Champion

The team will include many people from many departments who are also working on projects besides your joint venture. To keep this ball rolling, one person needs to coordinate. This person's job will be to stay on top of the process, to champion it from start to finish. He or she will need to call the meetings, keep the schedule, and do the myriad tasks, large and small, that coordinating a complex, cross-departmental project requires. Who your team captain/enterprise champion is will be crucial to the success of the project.

> Team captains must be creative and energetic: they should love the challenge of doing new things because they'll be writing the rules as they go along.

> Champions must be experienced at corporate politics: they'll have to know how to skirt the customary rules and how to convince key players to act.

> Team captains must be persuasive and respected: they'll have to defend the project to nay-sayers and sell it to fence-sitters.

> Champions must have clout: as they hunt for money and staff, they'll need management support to get what they need.

> Team captains need time to do the job: they should be freed from other tasks if necessary, because no one else has this as a top priority, and the project's momentum rides on their shoulders.

> Most of all, the team captains/champions should love the program. They must believe in it and its benefit to the company and community—in the long run enthusiasm is their best sales tool.

The Starting Lineup

While your strategic partnership initiative will benefit many parts of the organization, it must be managed by a relatively small group of people. These core players should represent the three functions that will be most directly involved: marketing, community relations, and human resources. (In some companies, one person may wear more than one of these hats.) With support from upper management, these people should be charged with developing a philosophy and setting the strategy in motion.

Who should the core players be? One or two people from each department will be adequate—but the choice of people is crucial. They should be high enough in the hierarchy to have discretionary power. You want decision-makers, not rubber-stampers; budget-controllers, not approval-seekers. When the team is in a room together, it must be able to make decisions—even financial decisions—without chains of approval above it. At least one person must have easy access to top management so when an executive decision is needed, it can be obtained quickly. These people must all believe in the program, and understand the "big picture" benefits to the corporation. They must want to be on the team and must be willing to give it the time it needs. They may need to be freed from some other responsibilities in order to do so, or at the very least the company needs to consider this project part of their normal business function.

The Bench

Your core team will need to bring in players from other departments at various stages in the process.

Initially, they'll need input from numerous people as they frame goals for the program. Every area that stands to benefit must be consulted. While the list will vary from corporation to corporation, it will probably include the basic "strategic family": customer relations (marketing and advertising), corporate contributions, government relations, investor relations, supplier relations, and distributor relations, in addition to the core members of the team mentioned earlier. It may also include representatives from new business development, research and development, and others. People from these departments should be involved in framing overall goals for the program, and in setting goals for individual campaigns that will benefit their departments.

Individual campaigns will involve other departments to greater or lesser degrees. A campaign that involves the company's sales force, franchisees, suppliers, and distributors will need representatives from the sales and purchasing departments. A campaign that links a new product or service with a nonprofit partner will involve representatives from new business development. Advertising and public relations people will join the team for most campaigns to plan ad and PR strategies. The core team must be free to call on players from other departments, such as people from communications, employee relations staff members, and brand managers, as their skills are needed, and as their departments stand to benefit.

Referee

Your corporate giving representatives should work most closely with your nonprofit partners. They are used to working with nonprofits—they speak their language, they understand their needs. They will be valuable brokers between the nonprofit's culture and yours. Take advantage of that. Let them take the lead in identifying nonprofits to work with. Let them make the initial contacts. Let them run the meetings at which both partners are present. Once you've developed working relationships with your nonprofit partners, that will no longer be necessary. But it's a good insurance policy in the early days of the program.

18

SETTING GOALS

"Corporate social responsibility efforts have several business related objectives: to foster goodwill while advancing business interest, to provide important demographic research and help develop markets, and to generate experience and build important networks in less familiar places and with new subject matter."

—*Global Corporate Citizenship Rationale and Strategies*
The Hitachi Foundation

<   <   <   <

One of the biggest dangers in strategic alliances involves setting goals. Invariably, people know who they want to work with and what they want to accomplish long before they have enough data to make those decisions.

This isn't about personal preference. It's about finding the right match between your company and your world. We've already shown you how many different parts of your company can benefit from getting involved in creating a joint effort. Each of those departments in your company has its own goals. Some of them overlap. And the perfect project is the one that can satisfy more than one goal.

For the sake of simplicity, let's assume that your company has five areas of interest: Marketing, New Business Development, Corporate Giving, Community Affairs, and Human Resources.

Your team should meet with representatives from each area to find out what their goals are. Marketing may be planning a new product launch, while Human Resources might be trying to develop an in-house day care center to give working moms a shot at making it work. Corporate Giving wants to spend money on kids, and New Business Development is trying to open new mar-

kets in the inner city. Suddenly, a pattern begins to form.
Let's look at each area one at a time.

Marketing Goals

To be candid, marketing drives most companies these days. It certainly
drives most strategic alliance efforts. So let's start there.

Your company has numerous marketing goals: overall company image,
products, services. You may market to a single consumer group or to several
groups with different characteristics. Each of these marketing goals has its own
challenges, and you'll need to decide which ones you want to tie to a campaign. For starters, look at each distinct group of marketing goals and ask yourselves the following questions:

1. *For each of our products or services...*
   > what geographic markets are we trying to reach?
   > what socioeconomic markets?
   > what gender?
   > what age group?
   > what life-style characteristics ?
   > what ethnic group?

   What other characteristics distinguish our target consumers?

2. *What are our goals for each of these target markets?*
   > to get them to try our product or service?
   > to encourage them to become or remain regular customers?
   > to encourage them to buy from our store, from other stores, by
     catalog, by phone?
   > to get them to tell friends about our product or service?

   What other goals do we have for our target markets?

3. *How do we want buyers to think about each of our products or services? What three words do we want them to associate with each product or service?*

4. *Where do we currently go to reach these people? Which campaigns
   have worked, and why? Which have failed, and why?*

5. *Do we have middlemen who help us get our product or service to the customer? If so, what are our goals for them?*
   > to get them excited about the product or service?
   > to get them to give us more space? More attention?
   What other goals do we have for them?

6. *How do we want people to think about our company? What five words do we want people to associate with us?*

Image

Image building is a major reason for embarking on a campaign. To have the most impact, you need to be very clear about what image you want to project. It will determine what social cause you adopt, whom you pick as a partner, and how you design the campaign.

Your company may have already determined its corporate image, as well as that of individual products and services. You may have an ad agency that has developed standards, slogans, and images to convey this image to the public. If so, review them. Do they mesh with the campaign goals and ideas you've generated? If so, how will you incorporate them into your plans? If not, how will you deal with the dissonance?

If you haven't already developed a clear corporate image, your "brand essence," take some time to do that now. How do you want your company perceived in three years? Did you list five words that describe your company when you were listing your marketing goals? If so, review them. Make sure everyone agrees. If you didn't make that list, do it now. Before you proceed with your campaign, you need to be able to define in five words, or one short sentence, the image it will convey.

Tying Marketing Goals and Image to a Strategic Partnership Initiative

A single campaign can't meet every goal, so you'll need to pinpoint which ones you want for this campaign. Three factors will help you decide: marketing needs with particular urgency, positive values your company wants to incorporate into its image, and the ease with which certain products or services lend themselves to this kind of campaign. Ask yourselves the following questions:

1. *Is there one product or service that could use a boost right now?*

Joint ventures can be a good way to focus attention on a particular product or service, so if one is lagging, this might be the way to give it a shove—especially if it has a natural fit with a social issue or a nonprofit.

> British Telecommunications (BT) is a leader in strategic alliances in the United Kingdom. In 1997 they gave £15 million to community causes, £150 million since they were privatized. In consumer polls in the United Kingdom they continually rank in the upper echelons of community service and commitment. Recently, as BT Phonecards prepared to introduce a new phonecard, they were faced with a need to phase out the old phonecards. In an innovative strategy, BT launched their "Give Them Shelter" promotion. For every old phonecard turned in, BT donates ten pence towards Shelter's "Winter Nights," with a minimum corporate donation of £100,000. British celebrities like Boy George and Leslie Ash have publicly supported the program. Not only did the program connect BT Phonecards with another worthy cause, but it also prepared the market for the new phonecards.

2. *Is there a particular value you'd like to attach to this campaign, something that you want the public to associate with you?*

It may be a general value like social responsibility, or trust, or respect. It could be something more specific, like the idea that JC Penney cares about kids and education.

> JC Penney often creates projects that help bolster a company's "positive image in customer's minds and help the company make a profit," according to Robin Caldwell, director of community relations. High school students and their parents represent a large segment of JC Penney's customer base. To let those customers know that JC Penney cares about their education, they offered eight $10,000 college scholarships. The applications for the scholarship competition were available at JC Penney stores, and every returned applica-

tion was rewarded with a t-shirt. To further enhance their image-building effort and increase their exposure to the target audience, JC Penney partnered with the Arizona Jean Company, a private brand, and advertised the promotion on MTV.

3. *Where is the best natural fit between your company and a social cause? Is it a single product or service? A line of products or services? Or the whole company's image?*

The disadvantage of tying a campaign to a single product or service is that the campaign will cost as much as a campaign that features an entire product line or the entire corporate image, making it less efficient as a marketing expense.

For a marketing partnership to work, the fit between the company and the cause must seem natural. There should be some logical, immediately apparent connection between your business and the work of your nonprofit partner. Like a loving marriage as opposed to an arranged one, a good joint venture can't be forced.

> The fit between Water 2000 and the Community Resources Group (CRG) is as clear as a cool mountain stream. In 1998 Water 2000 became the latest brand to jump into the bottled water pool with America's first "Socially Responsible" bottled water. Sold in Sam's Clubs around the country, Water 2000 donates a percentage of each sale to the Community Resources Group. CRG helps local groups with the issues of water supply and waste management. In fact, the Water 2000 project is the national name of a local project in Fayetteville, Arkansas. In Fayetteville, the water and the program are known as "In Our Backyard." The program's goal is to educate the public to the fact that, in America, more than a million people have no access to drinkable water. In addition to the sales of Water 2000/In Our Back Yard, when people in Fayetteville get oil changes, buy new cars, or fill prescriptions, a donation is made to the program. So far, $550,000 has been raised on the local level alone.

Philanthropic Goals

Your company's philanthropic goals may or may not play a significant role in shaping your strategic alliance program. If your company has a history of giving money, you probably already have standards in place for donations and existing relationships with nonprofits. You'll have to decide how much you want your program to be influenced by those relationships. You are not only free to make up new rules, but we strongly encourage you to go where no one in your company has gone before.

If your company does lack a systematic corporate giving strategy tied to business objectives, now is a good time to think about one. The following questions can help you structure both a philanthropic program and a joint venture:

1. *Is our philanthropy strategic?*
   > Is it done purely for social benefit, with no expected return to the company? Is it done with an eye on the corporate bottom line? Is it somewhere in between?

2. *To whom do we give money now?*
   > To what social causes?
   > To what nonprofits?
   > Do we have repeat recipients, or are all recipients new each year? How were these choices made?

3. *To whom do we want to be giving money? To what social causes? In what geographic region(s)? Are there specific nonprofits we've targeted? Why?*

4. *Is our philanthropy effective? Do we evaluate its results? Does it produce the desired benefit to the company and to the recipients?*

5. *Are there restrictions on using philanthropic dollars? What are they?*
   > Can we make our philanthropy more strategic within the limits of our restrictions?
   > Can we link it to our target markets?

> Can we involve our employees?

6. *What individuals must be involved in philanthropic decisions? How do they feel about strategic philanthropy and joint ventures?*

Human Resource Goals

Think of your campaign as a tool for building employee morale or providing employee benefits. The right project can give your workers a chance to participate in something fun, a chance to contribute to a social cause, and a chance to feel proud of their employer.

To make this kind of program work, though, you need to know two things: what causes your employees care about, and what activities they like. If the majority of your blue collar workforce likes baseball, don't create a program with the local ballet. And if your workforce is predominantly teenagers and unmarried adults, chances are a project targeted towards environmental issues will get a larger response than one targeted towards children's education.

This is where talking with human resources helps. HR knows your employees best, or at the very least, can get the answers you need. What social issues interest your workers? What activities do they enjoy? You're looking for an issue that engages employee interest, either because they care about it or because they enjoy participating in it.

To home in on the right issue, ask the following questions:

1. *What workplace issues are most pressing to employees? Which ones persist over time, and which will still be relevant in the next three to five years?*

2. *What social issues are most pressing to employees? Which ones persist over time, and which are likely to be relevant in the next three to five years?*

3. *Where do employees give time and money now?*
   > To what organizations do they belong?
   > For what organizations do they volunteer?

4. *Do we have an employee matching gift program? What organizations receive money?*

5. *Do we have an employee volunteer program?*
   > Where do employees volunteer?
   > Do they enjoy this?

6. *Do employees participate in "extracurricular" company events?*
   > What kind of events?
   > Do employees enjoy these?

7. *What skills do our employees have that would enable them to contribute effectively to a particular cause? What skills do you want them to acquire from volunteering for a cause?*

Community Affairs Goals

If your company is at all involved in community issues, whether locally, nationally, or internationally, you may want to think about linking those goals to your campaign. Some companies have taken up the banner of education and developed programs to strengthen local schools. Others have championed minority rights. Others have fought to keep a waste dump out of their town. Whatever the cause, you will be most effective if you pick one issue and put multiple corporate resources behind it. Working on several issues forces you to spread yourself too thin. If your joint venture can be matched to an issue you are already tackling, so much the better.

Once again, some targeting questions:

1. *With what issues is your company already involved?*
   > Environmental issues?
   > Political issues?
   > Economic issues?
   > Cultural issues?
   > Educational issues?
   > Minority issues?
   > Others?

2. *Do any of these issues lend themselves to a campaign?*

Issues that are highly controversial rarely make good marketing campaigns (although some companies like Benetton build their campaigns around controversy). In this case, controversial means at odds with the values and beliefs of your market, community, and corporate culture. Anti-smoking campaigns rarely fly at Phillip Morris. A pro-birth control fundraiser would be a tough sell among a conservative Catholic community.

Business Development Goals

Every business is involved in one or more of the following activities: developing new products or services, developing new markets, and improving relationships with suppliers and dealers. As you look ahead in your business, what new areas will you be moving into? A campaign can be used to attract new customers, to help you position yourself with future partners, to develop goodwill in future market areas, and to build relationships that can lead to new products or services.

To help you keep your growth plans in mind as you weigh the possibilities for a campaign, ask yourselves the following questions:

1. *What new markets has the corporation decided to target?*

2. *Any new products or services in development?*

3. *What are the company's research and development needs?*

4. *Are there universities or other nonprofits that might help?*

Listening to Your Lists

Congratulations. You're now the proud owner of a bunch of lists of answers to a bunch of questions. Now what?

Start by having your team captain/champion sum up each list on a separate sheet of paper. Then call a meeting of the team. At the meeting, compare the lists. Any target markets that show up on more than one list? Any social causes that repeat? Those are the areas that lend themselves most readily to a campaign. As you discuss the lists, weighing the needs of different departments, your goals will gradually become clear.

Guess what you do next? Make another list of all causes and organizations that showed up on the lists. Mark any that occur more than once. These are natural partners to consider as you develop a campaign.

Drafting a Strategic Alliance Philosophy

You've made lists. You've made lists of the common elements of those lists. Now comes an important moment. (No, it's not another list.)

As great as strategic alliances are, your program can't be all things to all people. It can meet numerous corporate goals, but ultimately it will meet some better than others. Your job now is to decide which ones. You need to draft a strategic alliance philosophy that will guide all your decisions from this point on.

> Will your program primarily be a marketing program? Will its first purpose be to increase sales, shelf space, inventory turnover, or other concrete measures of sales success? Will you design the program with those goals in mind? Will you expect it to perform like conventional marketing programs? When you evaluate it afterward, will you be disappointed if it doesn't measure up to those expectations?

> Or will the program be primarily an image program? Will its main intent be to refine the way the public thinks of you? As you design the program, will you emphasize the image-building aspects and sacrifice, if necessary, sales inducements, or social gain, or employee benefits?

> Or will your program be primarily philanthropic? Will its first purpose be to do some good for a social cause? To give back to your community? To make the world a better place? Are you willing to sacrifice some profit for the cause?

> Or will your program be somewhere in between? Do you want to increase sales and help a worthy cause, realizing that each goal may bend a bit in service to the other?

> Why is your company doing this? Is it a marketing technique that seems worth a try? Is it important to appear socially responsible? Is your company genuinely committed to helping the community?

There are no right answers to these questions. What's important is that you talk about them interdepartmentally—that you hear how various members of the company think, and learn what they expect, and that you come to a consensus. Build a coalition. While companies can say no to individuals, it's harder for them to say no to a coalition, especially one made up of their key players.

Your answers will be critical to the success of your program. They will determine how you design its elements, how you carry them out, and how you evaluate them afterward. If you can't agree now, you'll face unending conflict down the road—and few people will be happy with the outcome. If you agree on philosophy, you'll be able to design a program that meets the most needs, you'll be able to explain it convincingly to others, and you'll have solid ground for evaluating it once it's over.

19

PICKING A CAUSE

"[Our approach] is as much a part of our strategy in growing our business, as the products we select and carry. [It represents] a critical competitive advantage."

—*Suzanne Apple*
Home Depot
referring to Home Depot's commitment to community development
and youth-at-risk programs

<   <   <   <

Fill in the blanks:

Possible Social Causes Our Company Could Adopt:

1. My favorite causes:
   a.
   b.

Now that you've gotten that out of your system, we can go on.

The choice of social cause will be the single most important decision you make in your campaign. You want to make sure it's the right choice for your company—not just the right choice for you. That means you need to put more than personal preference into the decision—you need market research. You need to learn what social issues motivate your customers, potential customers, and employees. Then you'll know you've got a cause with charisma.

Market Research

So how do you find out what issues do motivate your customers, potential customers, and employees?

Research, research, research.

Within your company, it's easy. Ask them. Send out a memo. Add it to the company Web site. E-mail everyone. Put up suggestion boxes near the coffee machine. Run a contest.

Outside of your company the answers could be a little harder to come by. If your marketing department doesn't have existing demographic data, you'll have to find it, or create it. Your competition may be appealing to the same customer base. Look at what causes they're championing, and how success-fully their efforts are received by consumers. Check out the demographic data nonprofits have about their supporters.

But whether you're asking your employees or your customers, you have to ask the right questions. Find out what turns them on, what troubles them, which issues they support, which issues they find a waste of time. Make your questions specific. Within a cause there are subgroups, and you want to zero in as closely as possible on the issues that move your markets. Take the environment. Within that one area you've got animal-lovers and tree-huggers, people fighting pollution and people building nature trails, people saving local wetlands and people saving the Amazon rainforests. Which cause appeals to your audience? What geographic focus? For your campaign to be effective, you need to know the answers.

Ask each group which organizations they support. To what nonprofits do they belong? To which do they send money? For whom do they volunteer? You'll come away with a gold mine of information about your markets' pref-erences—and a list of possible causes and partners for your campaign.

When considering cause-related marketing for your company, there are a few persistent, observable, and quantifiable trends among your customers that support joint ventures:

The Purity and Simplicity Movement > This is the attitude you see in the return to virtue and value and the desire to recapture a more simple life. A good example of this movement is *The Book of Virtues* by William Bennet, former United States Secretary of Education.

Homesickness > This is a desire to simplify life and return to the time-less, the traditional, the original, and the authentic. For the company, the benefit of being associated with this trend is that it inspires trust.

Soft Social Activism > This is about making it easier for people to make a difference. It's important because your partnerships can provide your customers with the opportunity to do something unselfish, at little or no cost to them.

Vigilant Customers > The motto of these customers is, "I want to buy from a company that supports my values."

Following Up the Research

More than likely, your research will turn up several causes that interest your several audiences. That means you've got some choices. Your task is to narrow them down. (Make another, very short list.)

Do that by asking yourselves two important questions:

1. Which issue is closest to our field of business?
2. Which issue can we own?

Close to Your Business

It never ceases to amaze us how many companies still pick causes that have no connection to their business. It's great to want to "make a difference," but if you don't tie that effort to your own company's prosperity, it's much harder to justify and continue the effort.

Picking an issue that's close to your business is extremely important for several reasons.

First of all, you want to create a logical fit in consumers' minds. People should say, "Of course," when they hear what you're doing. That will help them remember. It will also make your efforts seem more credible. The Ronald McDonald Houses commitment to terminal children leaps to mind. As does Avon and Breast Cancer.

Second, you want a cause on which you can have an impact. When you choose an area related to your business, you already have contacts who can help. Your employees are informed and motivated. Your business associates can participate easily. One of the best examples of this is the Charge Against Hunger, a partnership between American Express and Share Our Strength, the anti-hunger group founded in 1984 by a group of chefs in Washington,

D.C. The Charge Against Hunger runs in restaurants that take the American Express card. In 1997, four years into the program, the program had generated over $21 million for Share Our Strength. During the campaign, American Express's 1997 fourth quarter profits jumped 15 percent.

Three, you want a cause that will motivate your customers. The closer the cause is to your business, the more persuasive it will be.

> Ralston Purina has created a successful campaign with the Humane Society featuring its lines of pet food. It is a classic cause-related marketing effort in which the company gives twenty cents to the Humane Society for every pet food coupon redeemed, up to a ceiling of $1 million. The money goes to a program called Pets for People, which helps seniors adopt pets. Ralston was shrewd in adopting the Humane Society. As a pet food manufacturer, the company could have said, "We're in the animal care business." That would have opened up a broad list of causes to support: animal rights groups, animal welfare groups, save-the-animal groups. But Ralston didn't say that. Instead, it zeroed in much closer to its customers. The company said, "We're in the pet food business. We want to reach pet owners. What causes appeal to them?" Defining its business—and its customers—narrowly led the company to the Humane Society's program. The resulting campaign has captured high visibility and approval with exactly the market Ralston wanted to reach. And it goes without saying that saving the lives of pets means more furry little mouths to feed.

Own Your Own

It is equally important to pick an issue you can own. As more and more companies get into strategic partnerships, it gets harder and harder to find a "new" issue. But try. Don't be a me-too player: be a leader. Pick an issue you can own, then stick with it. Your goal is to have an impact, to become identified with an issue and improve it. That's the way to build a reputation—not by spreading yourself too thin over a range of causes. The public won't remember if you've given a little to this cause, a little to that one, a little to the other.

Another reason to make sure you really own your cause is "ambushing," or the threat from competitors who steal your thunder. Remember American Express and the restoration of the Statue of Liberty? AmEx wasn't even a paid sponsor, but how many people can remember anyone else's involvement in the project?

Attention spans are too short. But the public will identify you with a cause if your joint venture is logical, long-term, and effective.

> > > >

Whew! You've accomplished a lot. By now, you've figured out the perfect cause for your joint venture. It's the cause that satisfied more of your company's goals than any other. It's got appeal to your employees and your customers. Now there's only one thing left to do: pick a nonprofit partner that deals with that cause. It should be easy, right? There are plenty of nonprofits to choose from.

As anyone familiar with the story "The Lady or the Tiger" knows, however, sometimes a beautiful lady is waiting behind the door, but, just as often, it's a man-eating tiger.

20

PICKING A NONPROFIT PARTNER

"I've grown up with organizations like the National Urban League and the American Red Cross, and I admire the work they've done. But unless they are working on one of our issues, we're not likely to support them."
— Paul Ostergard
VP/Director of Corporate Contributions
Citicorp

<   <   <   <

Working with a charity you believe in can make you feel all warm and fuzzy inside. But if it's the wrong choice for your company, that warm feeling may be all you get to keep on your way out the door. A logical connection is critical when picking both a social issue and the nonprofit partner with which to implement it. The right choice will attract the right audience and motivate it successfully. The wrong choice can turn people off or, worse, damage your reputation. How can you be sure to make the right choice? Measure each possible partner against the following criteria:

1. Pick a partner that matches your corporate image.
Even though the cause you pick matches your corporate image, it doesn't mean that the leading nonprofit in that field is the right match for your company. Countless projects have fallen short because the joint venture was based on access to target markets without concern for how they got that access. If you're trying to reach kids, don't partner with a comic book company or a cartoon unless you're prepared for the negative publicity associated with the medium.

And even within a single issue, different nonprofits have different images. Consider Greenpeace and the Nature Conservancy: both work to protect the environment, but one is seen as radical, the other as conservative. As a result, they attract different clienteles and would reflect differently on corporate partners. You can use this fact strategically to help shape your company's image. For example, look at how partnering different arts groups or healthcare agencies might reinforce your image:

> Do you want to be seen as strong, stable, and conservative? Pick a nonprofit with history and tradition—a museum, an orchestra, or an agency with a solid record in heart research or disaster relief.

> Do you want to be seen as adventuresome and pioneering? Partner with a newer organization recognized for experimentation—a contemporary arts center, an experimental theater, or an organization that works for people with AIDS or victims of domestic violence.

> Do you want to project an image of nurturing, warmth, and family values? Consider a children's museum, a zoo, or a children's hospital.

Each of these partners will help you attract a particular following, and each will project a certain personality. You'll be linking that personality to your own—so make sure it's the one your company wants.

2. Pick a partner that is credible in its field.

Your campaign will be only as strong as your nonprofit partner's reputation, so be sure to pick a partner that's everything it claims to be.

> Examine the nonprofit's track record. Has it had substantial accomplishments in its field?

> Examine its board. Is it governed by recognized experts?

> Examine its funding bases. Does it get grants from reputable sources?

> Examine its use of funds. Do they spend more money on programs, or on fundraising and administration?

Use experts in that area to help you pick a really solid partner. Don't rely on instinct—you may be an expert in your industry, but the nonprofit waters can be murky. Remember that American Express' relationship with Share Our Strength began when AmEx needed an expert to help them find the right recipients for their money.

3. Pick a partner that is financially and operationally sound.

You're not running a personality contest here; you're developing a business deal, and you need a partner you can depend on. They can lack funds, but they can't lack competence or integrity. To make sure you find one, examine the following:

The Organization's Size and Sophistication > Pick an agency that is well matched to your company. You want to look like partners—not like Mutt and Jeff.

The Organization's Financial Condition > Is it stable? Or will it need your venture to stay alive? Your partner may be saving a dying breed—but you don't want it to be one.

The Organization's Operation > Is it businesslike? Are the staff strategic thinkers? Do they meet deadlines? Ask for references from others who have worked with the organization. You want a business partner, not a protégé.

The Organization's Decision-Making Process > Is every decision a decision by committee? Can the organization develop systems for streamlining the process? Is the board involved in even minor decisions? This is potentially one of the trickiest areas in cause-related marketing. Flexibility on both sides will smooth the way considerably.

4. Pick a partner with a presence in the geographic area you want to reach.

People support causes that are close to home. Their loyalties are strongest to nonprofits in their own backyards. So when you pick a partner, pick one with a strong presence in the geographic areas you've targeted in your marketing plans.

> Are you creating a local marketing campaign? Pick a partner that targets the same area. It will give your campaign a hometown feel.

> Are you creating a regional campaign? Pick a nonprofit whose region corresponds to yours. Then work closely with it to tailor the campaign to regional interests.

> Are you creating a national campaign? Pick a nonprofit that operates nationally—it will reinforce your image across the country. But, if possible, work with the organization's chapters in different cities. Members and volunteers in those cities can be brought in to localize the campaign and give it a grass-roots character.

This idea is a tough one to swallow. We all want it to be true that a good idea in one part of the country is just as powerful in another. You can even try to make the case that "close to home" can have a philosophical meaning that overwhelms the geographic one. But think about AMFAR and AIDS. AMFAR, the American Foundation for AIDS Research may create national advertising campaigns, but it localizes those ads when it runs them. Helping the local AIDS clinic means helping your neighbors, not the nebulous "them" that often equates to "somebody else's" problem.

5. Pick a partner that will be yours exclusively.

In the same way that you want to own your issue, you want an exclusive relationship with your nonprofit partner. Try to avoid organizations that have participated in campaigns with many other companies. The public won't automatically associate them with you. It will be harder for you to have a demonstrable impact on the issue. And it will be harder to forge a long-term partnership or develop the sense of trust needed to reach your goal.

Instead, go for a nonprofit that's unattached. You'll be able to work with them to shape the campaign so that it meets your needs as well as the nonprofit's, without input from rival corporations. By finding your own nonprofit, you help draw more nonprofits into play, which is an important incentive in attracting the nonprofit community to get involved with the corporate world.

Also, make sure that they haven't left the back door open for your competitors to sneak in and ambush you while you're not looking. The road is littered with exclusive sponsors who were outdone by more glamorous donations and campaigns by their non-sponsor competition. (Again, think of American Express and the Statue of Liberty Restoration.)

6. Pick a partner you can work with.

Once you pick a partner, you're going to work with it for months or even years. Make sure you like it—its issue, its staff, the way they work and play. Make sure they like you. How do they feel about your business? Do they understand your needs? Or do they see you as a necessary evil on whom they must depend for needed funds?

This project should be fun for both of you. You want good chemistry between you. Remember, you're going to hit hard times—when your cultures clash, when you don't see eye to eye. That happens on every project, not just in co-ventures. But on most projects you don't get to pick your partners. Here you do. So do yourself a favor, pick one you like.

How to Not Pick a Partner

Occasionally, you may not want to pick a partner. That is, you may decide that as part of your strategy, you want to find a partner in an alternate way. For instance, you might want your customers to pick the partner, the way Working Assets does. Or you might want a panel of experts to pick the partner. Or you might avoid a single choice and instead pick several partners. All of these choices are fine—as long as they are made strategically.

Letting Your Customers Pick the Partner

Earlier we theorized that strategic partnerships are successful because they empower consumer choice. MasterCard took this empowerment a step further—they let their customers pick the cause.

> In 1987 MasterCard launched a campaign called Choose to Make a
Difference. Each time customers used MasterCard, the company
donated money to one of six national nonprofits: the American Heart
Association, Mothers Against Drunk Driving (MADD), the National
Committee for Prevention of Child Abuse, the Muscular Dystrophy
Association, the National Association on Drug Abuse Problems, and
AMC Cancer Research Centers.
    The choice to include six nonprofits was made in response to
market research. Studies showed that baby boomers wanted to give
to charity, but didn't want to feel the sting. They also wanted to
decide which charities they supported. So MasterCard designed its
campaign accordingly, polling consumers to learn which charities
were of greatest interest to them. MasterCard built its campaign
around the "winners" and around consumers' ability to choose
between them.
    Did market research pay off? It did. The campaign raised $2.8
million for the six charities—and boosted MasterCard use by 19 percent. According to consumer surveys, it also gave MasterCard a better image than Visa for the first time ever.

The key here is making the customer's choice central to the campaign. If
you want to use this approach:

> Build your campaign around the fact that customers get to choose.
Include that fact in all campaign ads and literature. Make the customers' choice the selling point of the campaign.

> In a local campaign with small donations, you can let your customers
choose freely. However, in a regional or national campaign, or in a
campaign with sizable donations, you should preselect a small number of recipient organizations. Otherwise, the number of choices
made by customers will be unmanageable. Make sure your prese-
lected choices meet all the criteria for partnership—and that all of
them fit under the umbrella of the issues your company can support.

> Publicize the results. In a local campaign with many recipients, publicize the list of recipients. Take out a full-page newspaper ad, post the list in your store, or mail the list to your clients. It's important for people to know their contributions were received and their voices were heard. In regional or national campaigns with predetermined recipients, publicize the results of the customer "vote." Let customers know how much money they channeled to each organization so they can feel good about their participation. Remember the survey data we presented in chapter 3? An increasing percentage of consumers feel failure to publicize results points to questionable business practices.

Letting a Panel of Experts Pick the Partner

American Express used this approach in a cause-related marketing campaign called Project Hometown America. The company wanted a campaign with a grass-roots personality. So it decided to contribute money to small organizations working in cities across America to improve their local communities. Rather than pick the many recipients itself, the company created a board of advisers made up of volunteers from organizations across the country. These people were qualified judges of local organizations, and better able to make the selections than the company would have been. An added benefit is the "celebrity endorsement" factor of the judges. Even if they're not actually celebrities, their expertise and qualifications will bring added value to your campaign.

If you want to use this approach:

> Make sure your panel is well qualified. Its members will reflect on your organization every bit as much as their choices, so they should also meet the criteria for strategic partners.

> Establish clear criteria for recipient organizations. Publicize those criteria so that customers know what types of organizations will be chosen.

> Publicize the panel and its decision-making process. Make sure the process is straightforward and aboveboard.

> Publicly celebrate the winners. Let people know where their money has gone.

Picking Several Partners

The danger in picking several partners is that it violates a very basic marketing rule: keep it simple. With multiple partners you run the risk of having your campaign appear unfocused. You also have more relationships to manage. If you decide to partner several nonprofits, try the strategy Johnson & Johnson used in its "Shelter Aid" campaign (chapter 5). The company had multiple nonprofit recipients but only one cause. In effect, the cause itself became the partner.

If you want to use this approach:

> Pick nonprofits in a related field. You might pick a few environmental, healthcare, or arts organizations. Regardless of how many you actually pick, keep them all within a single cause.

> Keep the overall number of nonprofits small. You want to have an impact on the issue. The fewer partners you have, the more money and help you will be able to give each one. And again, the fewer partners, the easier the project will be to coordinate and manage.

> Make sure all the organizations meet your criteria for partners. One inappropriate partner can unhinge the entire campaign.

21

GETTING EMPLOYEES ON BOARD

"When we create a desirable workplace and find good ways to have work/life balance, we'll attract and we'll retain the best people—and that's our competitive advantage."

— *Lewis Platt*
CEO, *Hewlett-Packard Co.*

<   <   <   <

One of the biggest reasons to embark on a strategic alliance initiative is to boost employee morale. That means employees should be involved in shaping and implementing the campaign from the beginning. You want them to feel some ownership of the program, not that it is a *fait accompli* handed down from above. We've already described how to work with your human resources people to plan employee involvement. They're the ones to tell you how to design the campaign to best meet employee needs.

Employees can feel involved even if they never participate in the project, just by being kept informed. They perceive their company as doing something important, which improves how they feel about the company. There's also the possibility that people who wouldn't volunteer on their own will jump on the bandwagon as it picks up speed. Remember the survey data that shows that employees want to work for a company that's doing good, and feel better about themselves when they do.

Maximizing Employee Satisfaction

Communicate Strategically > As you plan your communications package, don't forget your employees. Think of them as an audience to be communicated with the same way you think about external markets.

Solicit Employee Input > Your employees are a resource for feedback. Don't let that resource go unused. Create two-way channels for communicating about the campaign. Appoint an "answer person" for the campaign—someone employees can go to with comments or questions. Then take their comments seriously. Revise the campaign from time to time in response to their suggestions—and let them know you did. The more ownership they feel, the more benefit you will derive.

Use Multiple Media > Use a variety of media to tell employees about the campaign: in-house newsletters, Web sites and e-mail, bulletin boards, staff meetings, suggestion boxes—whatever vehicles you generally use for communicating with workers. The more you talk to them about the campaign, the more seriously they will take it.

Start Early > Don't wait until you launch your campaign to tell your employees you're doing it. They'll know you're thinking about it because, presumably, you've asked them about causes and nonprofits they support. Tell them the results of your market research. As you narrow the field to a few causes and a few nonprofits, ask them their opinions. If you keep them involved throughout the process, they'll feel greater ownership once the campaign is announced.

Keep Them Informed > Before you launch any aspect of the campaign, and before you leak any news to the press, be sure your employees know. Don't set them up to be surprised when stories break. They should feel like insiders—after all, this is their campaign, too. You don't want them to be embarrassed if a customer or a friend asks them about the campaign and they don't know anything. Your employees are ambassadors to the outside world. Make sure they're well-briefed.

Showcase Employee Involvement > As employees get involved in the campaign—whether through volunteering, donating, or working on the campaign itself—place stories about their involvement in both in-house and external media. The publicity will make them proud and will encourage others to get involved, too.

Be Clear > Make the terms of employee involvement clear. Is it mandatory? Does it have an impact on evaluations? Will employees be penalized for not participating? We suggest the answer to these questions be "No"—but employees may not know that. Make it clear.

Showcase Management Support > Support for your campaign must start at the top, and employees need to know it's there. Have top executives address staff meetings. Have them write stories in the newsletter. Have them volunteer for the nonprofit to set an example. Use whatever means work in your corporate culture to let management express its belief in the program. Employees want to know that the program is heartfelt and long-term. It will be hard for them to take it seriously if they think the big guns don't care.

Involving Your "Middlemen"

All the rules that apply to involving employees apply equally to involving "middlemen"—your sales force, your franchises, your distributors, anyone you count on to get your product or service to the public. These people can often make or break a campaign by lending or withholding their support. Make sure they like the campaign. Get them involved at the beginning, so they can see the project develop rather than have to digest it from out of nowhere. As the project grows, they can gauge its impact on their jobs, better preparing for their role and even finding ways they can use your project to increase their own profits and involvement. Remember, they're business people too: if you want to make money while making a difference, wouldn't they?

Do Market Research > When you poll customers and employees about what causes and nonprofits they support, poll your middlemen, too.

Solicit Their Input > Appoint someone to be the communications link with these people and make sure they solicit input on a regular basis. Your middlemen are closer to the action than you are in your corporate offices. They also know their territories better than you do. Give them a hand in shaping the program so that it will work on their turf. Then solicit and respond to their feedback once the campaign is in action.

Keep in Touch > Use a campaign newsletter or other vehicle to communicate with them regularly. Give them the big picture of the campaign so they know what to expect and regular updates to let them know what's happening. Include stories from middlemen in your communications. They're close to the action, so they should have good stories. You'll be recognizing their involvement, and nearly everybody loves to be written about in a positive light.

Emphasize Home Team Support > Make it clear that the home office is serious about the program. It will be tough for your middlemen to get behind it if it seems like a flaky idea from headquarters that might be abandoned any month. Remind them regularly that the campaign is here to stay and that top management is committed.

Introduce Your Partner > Your middlemen may be working with your partner's local chapters to implement the campaign. Smooth the way by giving them as much information as possible ahead of time. Brief them about the nonprofit. Warn them about possible culture clashes. Make sure they clearly understand your goals as well as your partner's. Pass on any tips you've learned from your dealings with your partner that might foster a good working relationship. The more smoothly those two groups get along, the better the campaign will run.

22

DEVELOPING A CAMPAIGN

"Nothing is more dangerous than an idea when it is the only one you have."
— *Emile Chartier, French philosopher*

<   <   <   <

You've set your goals. You've picked an issue. You've thought of partners. By now, you've probably got ideas for campaigns you'd like to launch. It's time to shake some hands and sign some contracts, right?

Wrong. Before you approach a prospective partner, you need something with which to approach them: a package of solid venture ideas. You'll refine these ideas later, with your partner. But first you need to develop a package that works for you and that your partner can respond to. That means you need a campaign brainstorm. Why brainstorm new ideas when you already have several you like? For a number of reasons.

> You want to avoid the trap of falling in love with your first idea. How do you know there isn't a better idea waiting to be discovered? Or a cluster of good ideas that you can carry out in combination? Unless you probe a bit, you'll never know what you're missing. You may well come back to the idea you started with. But if you do, you'll know for sure that it's the right one.

> You really want more than one idea. Your campaign will be strongest if it includes several separate, related ventures which can be rolled out in conjunction with each other. These will keep the program fresh in the public eye, give people numerous ways to get involved, and extend the program's life. Brainstorming will help you find a number of ideas you like, instead of just one or two.

> You need several good ideas with which to approach a nonprofit. The nonprofit's staff will want to feel that they can help shape the program, not that they're being offered a single idea, take it or leave it. There's also a secret many advertising agencies have learned: even though you know you have a winning idea, presenting more than just that one idea gives them room to have something they can hate. It's just the reality that some clients need to trash something in order to feel that they've done their job. Going in with more than one idea often means your good idea comes back out alive. (Note: Don't bring in any bad ideas—the way things work out, they're often the ones that get bought.)

> Ultimately, you will work with your nonprofit partner to develop the campaign. The nonprofit will be an equal player in the venture, so the staff will get equal say in what you do. If you spend time brainstorming ventures now, you'll go into those negotiations with a list of projects that meet your needs.

> Finally, brainstorming is fun. It's a freewheeling, no-holds-barred session in which you sit around a table, shouting, gesticulating, and interrupting each other while you think of all the ventures you could possibly do. Goofy ones. Serious ones. Great but impractical ones. Out of the mix will come more solid ideas than you'll actually be able to use. So roll up your sleeves. Pour the coffee. And dig in.

The Brainstorming Session

Your brainstorming session should be attended by everyone on the core team, as well as a few individuals chosen specifically for their creativity. These can be company insiders or complete strangers to the business. They can be people from your ad agency, if you have one and really like the way they think. The key requirement is that they be truly creative—that they be freethinkers who can take an idea and run with it. Keep the total number of brainstormers to ten or less.

We suggest that you hold the meeting in the morning when everyone is fresh. If possible, hold it first thing in the morning, before people have gone to their desks. You want them to be clear-headed, not distracted by today's concerns. Allow two hours—no more, no less. Two hours gives you enough time to warm up, get goofy, get serious, get ideas flowing, and then quit before you burn out.

A few days before the meeting, it's a good idea to circulate a two-page paper to all attendees explaining the reason for the meeting, the goals of the campaign, and the image words or slogan you've agreed on. Include background information on the issue you've chosen and on your nonprofit partner, if you've picked one. A brochure from the partner would be best.

On the day of the meeting, consider going into the conference room ahead of time with a pad of large sheets of paper. Label each sheet with one of the options described in Part II—cause-related marketing, premiums, sponsorships, licensing, sponsored ads, and so on—and one sheet marked "Other." Tack your sheets on the walls: you'll want to fill them with ideas before the meeting is through. (It may seem as though we're being prescriptive in terms of "how to do" something that's supposed to be free form. But decades of combined experience have proven the power of big sheets of paper as an aid to a successful brainstorming session.)

Designate one person—possibly the team captain—as the meeting's official facilitator and recorder. This person's job is to ask the questions, keep the meeting going, and take notes. The person you designate has to be a good listener. They'll do more writing than talking.

Start the meeting by going over the "givens"—the campaign goals, the social issue you've picked, your nonprofit partner, the image you want to project. Don't spend a lot of time, just make sure everyone's up to speed. Then, one by one, take up each of the campaign strategies listed on the walls around you. Ask yourselves: What kind of cause-related marketing campaigns could we do that would meet our goals, work well with our prospective partner, and be fun and interesting to the public and the media? What kind of special events? What kind of premium items? What kind of sponsored ads?

Take the strategies one at a time. Try to milk each one for all it's worth before going on to the next. The idea is to get as many ideas out as you can. Don't worry about quality. Quantity is what counts. Dumb ideas will lead to good ones. The point is to generate ideas that would never arise under more "orderly" circumstances.

When discussion starts to flag, move on to the next strategy. (But not until then. The surest way to kill somebody's desire to play is to shut them up while they still have something to say.) If an idea doesn't fit a strategy, put it on the sheet called "Other." If the conversation takes you back to an earlier sheet, go with it. If you fill up a sheet, tape another one right on top. The goal is to fill as much space on the walls as possible.

The process will start slowly, but by the end of two hours you should have generated a lot of heat, a lot of paper, and a lot of ideas. You'll have silly ones, impractical ones—but also a lot of good ones—ideas you never would have thought of had you stopped after your first few thoughts. Later you'll evaluate them all. For now, give yourselves a big pat on the back, take a deep breath, and go back to your real jobs.

Post-Brainstorm Evaluation

Now that you've done the fun work, you need to do some serious work. You must evaluate all the ideas you came up with and decide which ones are worth pursuing. Some you'll discard immediately. Some will seem iffy. Some will seem downright doable. Narrow the list to ten or fewer and measure each of those against the following criteria:

Goals > Does this idea meet at least one, and preferably more, of your stated goals? If not, lose it. You're not doing this campaign for brownie points. You're doing it for both corporate and social payback.

Fit > Is there a logical fit between this idea, your products and/or services, the social cause, and the nonprofit partner? If not, the public won't buy it.

Simplicity > Is the idea simple and easy to understand? Can you explain it in one sentence? Do people respond, "Gee, I wish I'd thought of that!"? If not, it's probably too complex and the public won't get it.

Appeal > Will it interest your target market? Do market research to test the idea. If it doesn't fly, forget it.

Newsworthiness > Will it attract specialty media that reach your target markets? Will mass media pick it up? In today's era of twenty-four-hour, voracious news outlets, the media is desperately hungry and frequently bored. Pique the interest of a jaded reporter, and you'll probably get the chance to pique the interest of the public. If you can, test the idea on friends in the media to see if they like it as much as you do.

Longevity > Will it sustain the public's interest for as long as it needs to? Or will it get old before its time?

Ownership > Will your company be able to "own" the program in the public's mind? If you can't get an exclusive—at least in your own industry—rethink the program, the cause, and the partner.

Merchandising Potential > Are there merchandising opportunities attached to this idea? Can you create point-of-purchase displays? Discount coupons? In-store events? Souvenir products? What additional revenue generators can be attached to the campaign?

Cost-Effectiveness > Is this a good use of your dollars? Or would you get as much return by spending them in a different way? (This one's killed more good ideas than almost any other criteria. And it should. Remember, this is about making money… while making a difference.)

Employee Appeal > Will your employees respond? Can they participate?

Middleman Support > Will retailers, distributors, salespeople, and anyone else you depend on to get your products or services to the public respond to it? You may be counting on them for support. (Don't let this one kill an idea that's passed the other criteria. Sometimes, a little hand holding, a little education, and a little bit of throwing your muscle around can help your middlemen see the light.)

Management Support > Will management get behind it in a big way? If not, better not do it. But if you can sell management on the idea, if they understand the power of this radical approach to doing business, then they will be an invaluable support to you as you rewrite the rules.

Any venture idea that passes these criteria packs a lot of potential.

23

ONE-SHOT CAMPAIGNS VS. MULTI-LAYERED VENTURES

"We are known as a company that gives. We are looking for something long-term. We are looking for something deeper."
—*Lori Hand*
Director of National Promotions and Publicity
Starbuck's

<   <   <   <

Once you've evaluated each idea, you'll have a short list of projects with big potential. Your next task is to think about how to turn those ideas into a campaign. You have two options. One is to pick out your favorite and run with it: you can do a one-shot event, hope it's a big success, then think about venture number two. Good plan. We've presented plenty of examples of highly successful one-shot campaigns, like American Express's Statue of Liberty restoration or Kellogg's cause-related marketing project with the March of Dimes.

Your second option is to do a multi-layered campaign in which you and your nonprofit partner enter into several ventures together, rolling out one after another, over a longer period. A perfect example of this longer-term option is what Pillsbury did with their Pillsbury's Customer Community Partnerships, or American Express does with Share Our Strength. This is an even better plan, although there are pros and cons to both arrangements. According to surveys like the 1996 Cone/Roper survey, executives are trending away from tactical one-shot ventures and toward longer-term CRM that is more highly integrated into their basic business goals.

The One-Shot Campaign

The main advantage of a one-shot campaign is that it's easy. You and your nonprofit partner agree on a venture you would like to pursue, you implement the campaign, and you're done. At that point you can sit back, evaluate the results, and decide whether you want to do more. No muss. No fuss. No long-term commitment. If you had a difficult working relationship, or if you've discovered that CRM partnerships don't suit your company, you can exit gracefully.

One-shot campaigns are an excellent way to get started in partnering. They give both partners a chance to test the waters, learn about each other, learn about the process, and then decide whether and how to proceed. They are definitely recommended for beginners. Also, in many companies that live or die on quarterly bottom lines, a short term, one-shot campaign is the only one you can sell to upper management. At least to start with.

The disadvantage of one-shot campaigns is that they don't take maximum advantage of a corporate-nonprofit joint venture. You've gone to the trouble of picking a cause, learning how to work with each other, positioning yourself in the public mind—and then it's all over in a flash. There's no continuing public reminder. No continuing consumer interaction. No continuing glory. A far more effective way to build a campaign is to design it for a longer term. That produces greater gain for the corporation, for the nonprofit, and for the cause.

Advantages of Multi-Layered Ventures

In a multi-layered campaign, the corporation and the nonprofit plan a package of ventures. Each venture is related to the others and rolls out according to a preset timeline. Each venture reinforces the others, and each offers the public a different way to get involved.

There are numerous advantages to this arrangement:

Ownership > A multi-layered campaign cements your co-venture in the public mind. The variety of events and continuing nature of the campaign constantly remind the public that you are working together.

Longevity > A multi-layered campaign can keep the relationship in the public eye for an extended period. With new events constantly emerging, it remains continually fresh.

Commitment > By building a long-term, multi-pronged relationship with the nonprofit, you affirm your company's commitment to its cause. Your actions say, "We genuinely care about this issue, we're not just here to make a buck."

Continuing Benefit > A multi-layered campaign enables you to benefit from continuing progress in your adopted cause. For instance, if a breakthrough is made in medical research that your campaign helped fund, you'll still be in the limelight when the breakthrough happens. If your campaign raises money for a new building for your partner, you'll still be there to bask in the glory when the building opens. Think of the alternative as pumping money into a slot machine for hours and then leaving while the very next person hits the jackpot.

Maximum Impact > A multi-layered campaign produces maximum gain for your partner and allows you to have maximum impact on the cause. Because your partner is showcased repeatedly to the public, it has many chances to broadcast its message; consumers have many chances to learn about the organization and get involved. Plus, in a multi-layered campaign you can offer more than money to the cause. You can use your employees to lend manpower. You can use your contacts with decision-makers to influence policies. You can give in-kind donations of equipment you no longer need. Each new offering can become a new element in your campaign, giving you numerous ways to keep the campaign fresh without spending more money.

Maximum Impact, Period > We liked the last one so much, we wanted to repeat it. Targeting one issue with a variety of corporate resources will have much more impact on the issue—and on the public—than spreading your resources over several issues. A multi-layered campaign is the best way to do that.

Of course, there's a down side to all this. A multi-layered campaign is more expensive to produce than a one-shot deal. The timing and coordination are more complex. It takes time and effort to keep the elements running smoothly. And it requires a good working relationship between the partners. But those things are manageable—and often get easier as a campaign unfolds.

Just take the issue of working relationships. In a one-shot campaign, the personnel involved take on a high level of importance. In some companies, the projects even become, "Debbie's pet project" or "That thing Barry's doing." And a personnel conflict can sink even the best project—the tales of disaster are endless. But in a long term, multi-layered campaign, the importance of the project becomes paramount. A single employee can't outweigh the mountain of previous effort or the history of the project.

Other aspects of strategic alliances become easier, too. Initial budgets can be hard to sell to upper management, but ongoing funds are just a continuation of an existing budget item, a much easier sell in many corporations.

For these reasons and many others, we recommend that you develop a package of ventures that can be combined into a multi-layered campaign— but that you execute only the first. After it's over, sit back and evaluate it. Did it do what you wanted? Did you like your partner? If yes, you're on a roll, bring out the rest of the package. If not, shake hands and say good-bye. You can try again in the future.

Time Frame

As you plan your multi-layered campaign you'll need to determine several things: the life span of each individual event, the spacing of the events, and the duration of the entire campaign.

Individual Event Lifespans

Individual events tend to suggest their own duration. A special event such as a concert may last only two hours, with attendant promotion stretching out to a month. A campaign may last three months. Most events have a natural life span which you should respect. However, keep in mind as you plan that short-term events may cost almost as much as medium- or long-term events, but give the public a much shorter time to respond. By the same token, events that last longer than three months may get stale as their novelty wears off.

Event Spacing

When you plan the spacing of individual events within a multi-layered campaign, think about the pacing of the overall campaign. You may want some events to roll out rapidly to build impact. Others may happen slowly, with a lag of as much as six months in between. Your goal is to maintain an element of surprise: the public should never know what's coming next—or when it will come. As you plot a timeline for the campaign, keep in mind the public's attention span, internal events in both organizations that may affect your ability to implement the campaign, and events in the outside world with which you may want to affiliate, or which you may want to avoid.

Campaign Duration

How long should a multi-layered campaign last? It depends—on the relationship between the partners, on the urgency of the cause, on the receptivity of the public. Numerous factors determine the best length for a campaign. A campaign can potentially last for years. As mentioned earlier, Texaco has partnered the Metropolitan Opera since 1940. Procter & Gamble has partnered the Special Olympics since 1981. As long as the joint venture continues to satisfy both partners, why not keep it going? The important thing is to evaluate it regularly in order to know how well it's performing. Here are some things to look for:

Effectiveness > Is the campaign working? Is it producing the results you anticipated? If not, there's not much point in keeping it around, unless you can fix it to get the results you want. See chapter 27, "Evaluating Your Campaign," for tips on determining its effectiveness.

Public Perception > Is the public still excited? Don't let the campaign overstay its welcome. Everything gets tired after a while, so you want to watch for early warning signs of campaign fatigue. It's better to end a campaign early while public enthusiasm is still high than hang on too long. You can always bring it back later: people will be delighted to see an old friend return. But an event that has stayed too long will be dead forever. Use market research throughout the campaign to stay in touch with public perception. That way you'll always know what to do. (In your research, be sure to distinguish between the entire multi-layered campaign and individual campaign elements. The public may grow tired of a single element without tiring of the entire campaign.)

Partner Satisfaction > Are you still enjoying the campaign? Is your partner? If dissatisfactions are overtaking benefits, it's time to call a halt. Your campaign management will suffer if you're not having fun. Find an issue and a partner you'll enjoy.

Issue Urgency > Is the issue still pressing? Very occasionally, social issues disappear because major strides are made. If that happens on your issue, great! Declare victory and move on to a new cause. But don't expect it to happen. Most issues are ineradicable. Your goal should be to adopt an issue for the long term and really make a difference. Be wary of being faddish. If you move from one issue to another, constantly looking for the most popular cause, you'll be branded insincere.

Test Market Your Campaign

Most companies test market a new product before rolling it out in a full-scale launch. If you're planning a national campaign, consider test marketing it, too. Testing lets you gauge the public's interest. Equally important, it enables you to work out the bugs before going national. Pick one city for your trial. Work closely with your retailers, salespeople, or other "middlemen," and with your partner's local chapter (if it has one) to plan and execute each element. Then evaluate carefully. You'll gain important information that can influence the rest of the campaign.

First Brands, manufacturer of Glad Bags, has done a multi-year campaign with Keep America Beautiful (KAB). Called the Glad Bag-a-thon, the campaign was introduced to highlight Glad's new Handle-tie trash bag. The idea behind the campaign was that citizens in local communities would take a day to clean up their city, using, of course, Glad Handle-tie bags. To test the idea, First Brands partnered with five KAB chapters in five cities. That gave them a chance to learn how to work with KAB and how to organize an event that depended quite literally on the kindness of strangers. The following year the company took the campaign national.

24

BUDGETING FOR A JOINT VENTURE

"It is possible… to make a big impression without a lot of money. No won-der so many of us are flocking to cause marketing."

—*David D'Alessandro*
President/COO
John Hancock Mutual Life Insurance Co.

< < < <

What does a joint venture cost? Obviously, the costs vary enormously, depend-ing on scale, duration, number of elements, and a host of other factors. Strategic alliance initiatives tend to cost about the same amount as traditional sales promotions, with a donation to the nonprofit sometimes added to the mix. Your other costs—developing the campaign, creating materials, buying media, doing market research, and so on—remain essentially the same.

The donation to the nonprofit, in fact, represents the smallest part of the total expense. In 1989 Smirnoff Vodka donated $100,000 to Literacy Volunteers of America as part of a sponsored advertising campaign. The com-pany then spent ten times that amount—$1 million—to promote the cam-paign. Smirnoff spent that much on promotion to maximize the campaign's visibility. Most companies spend two to three times the donation amount on advertising and promotion. And they consider it money well spent. After all, that's how they tell the world what they're doing. United Technologies, for example, allots a generous promotion budget to each of its arts sponsorships because, as C.R. Hogan Jr., manager of corporate contributions, says, "We look at it as the best way of protecting our investments in these organizations."

Another way to look at the donation is as a licensing fee. Many companies have no problem paying fees to engage in licensed promotions: tie-ins with movies, comic books, cartoons, sport stars, etc. As licensed promotions continue to grow as a percentage of all promotions, the fees are skyrocketing. It's not unheard of for a licensor to charge $1 million just for the use of their characters or likeness, above and beyond actual costs for premiums and appearances. And when it's over, those companies don't retain any special benefit from their use of the icon, which has gone on to sell some other product a week later. Compared to these numbers, and given the image-building a well-conceived campaign can create, it's easy to think of the donation as a licensing fee to the angels.

Which Pot to Pick?

One of the advantages of campaigns is that companies have a wide range of choices when it comes to finding the funding. Money can come from the corporate giving budget as well as any number of business budgets. Most companies pull dollars from a variety of budgets, depending on which departments plan to benefit and which have the most to spend.

Money from the corporate giving budget is tax-deductible, which can be an incentive for companies that don't want to spend business dollars and want the deduction. However, money from business budgets is essentially tax-deductible as well, since it, too, comes out of earnings. Therefore, deductibility itself need not influence your funding decision.

Since we're talking about changing the way companies look at strategic alliances by giving example after example of increased sales due to these efforts, we fully expect to see an increase in the use of marketing dollars to fund these efforts. Frankly, it's easier to justify marketing dollars, anyway. Philanthropic spending is by definition less interested in increasing company earnings. Our premise is that marketing dollars spent in cause-related marketing can yield greater profits than marketing dollars spent in other ways, when done properly.

Cautions

Two other concerns should influence your thinking. The first is that the source of funds can place additional pressure on the project to succeed if other programs suffer as a result. Therefore, it's wise to consider the potential backlash as you decide who's going to foot the bill.

The second is that corporate philanthropy money often has strings attached that may influence how the money is spent. Most corporate foundations are prohibited from self-dealing: their money must be spent on educational programs rather than programs that directly benefit the business. Companies deal with this restriction by using philanthropic money to donate to the nonprofit but using marketing funds to create the promotional elements of the campaign.

General Rules for Budgeting

One of the hardest things about budgeting for a strategic partnership campaign is the lack of certainty. Since you've never done it before, it's hard to know what you're getting into. Unexpected costs will no doubt crop up. It's best to think of strategic alliances the way you would any new program: you give it your best guess and then prepare for the worst. We offer the following two crucial bits of advice:

Give Yourself Room > Take the program seriously and allocate a large enough budget to make it a significant part of your overall marketing program. Give it the advertising and promotional support it needs. Don't inhibit its chance to fly by clipping its wings at the start.

Give Yourself Flexibility > As we've said before, there is no "right way" to do strategic alliances. Most successful examples of joint ventures have broken new ground. The only sure thing about a campaign is that it will cost more than you thought. Plan for contingencies. Give yourself room to make mistakes, to change your mind, to realize halfway through that there's a better way to do things. These flip-flops may be costly in the short term. But they'll pay off in the ultimate success of the program. Certainly they'll pay off in future campaigns, since you'll enter those with valuable experience under your belt.

25

"We think we can bring our expertise in advertising and promotion to bear in helping to achieve broader societal goals."
—*Robert M. Viney*
Associate Advertising Manager for Environmental Marketing Policy
Procter & Gamble

<   <   <   <

Money may make the world go around, but to a nonprofit many other things can be almost as helpful. As mentioned earlier, corporations have a wealth of non-monetary assets that can be valuable to a nonprofit partner. Lending or donating those items can extend your campaign, giving it longer life in the public eye. In Part II we examined the variety of in-kind donations a company can make. This chapter will help you locate donatables within your company, and suggest ways to incorporate them into a campaign.

Employee Volunteers

We're not talking about employee involvement in your end of the CRM venture. We're talking specifically about encouraging your employees to volunteer for your partner, as we showed earlier in the examples from EDS, Marks & Spencer, and IBM Deutschland. Lending out your employees to partners creates a win-win-win situation. The nonprofit gets needed manpower, as well as valuable skills it may be missing. The employee gets a chance to contribute directly to a social cause and to develop skills they may not use at work. The company benefits from the employee's development and improved morale, as with Marks & Spencer, as well as the potential to develop new products, as was the case with IBM Deutschland.

Volunteering can happen at either the management or employee level. Employees provide much-needed manpower to a nonprofit. They are especially valuable if they volunteer regularly and get to know the organization. Managers can be equally valuable because they can be lent for their specific skills. Does your partner need help with accounting? Lend someone in your business office for two hours a week who can help strengthen the system. Does your partner need help with marketing? Put your marketing manager on call for ten hours a month to help develop a marketing plan.

To implement this, you could circulate a survey asking employees about their volunteering preferences. What kinds of agencies would they like to work for? What kind of work would they like to do? How much time could they spend? What skills do they have that they would like to use in a volunteer capacity?

In-Kind Donations

As we said in chapter 11, things that you take for granted may be extremely valuable to your nonprofit partner. In casting about for possible in-kind donations, ask yourselves three questions:

1. *What are we throwing away?*

   Are you redoing your offices? Installing new equipment? Discarding reject product? Ask whether your partner can use your throwaways. Many a nonprofit is furnished, equipped, or fed with corporate discards.

2. *What services do we perform in-house that we could also perform for our partner?*

   Do your in-house facilities sometimes have down time? Would your employees enjoy tackling a new and different project? Find out whether your partner can use those services. Possibilities include printing facilities, delivery and transportation facilities, warehousing facilities, photographic or videotaping services, art direction or production services, copywriting services, data processing services, and research services.

3. *Can our partner use our commercial product or service?*

Is the product or service you sell something your partner can use? Do you have overstock? Seconds? Products that have been replaced by newer versions? Companies that donate current inventory to non-profits are eligible for a "stepped up" tax donation. Companies that donate services can take tax deductions for out-of-pocket expenses. Consider using a clearinghouse, such as Gifts in Kind America in Alexandria, Virginia, or the National Association for the Exchange of Industrial Resources (NAEIR) in Galesburg, Illinois. They can arrange single donations or develop a turnkey giving program for you.

Facility Use

Does your company have facilities it doesn't use all the time that might be useful to your nonprofit partner? Possibilities include vans, office space, conference rooms, and warehouses. A real estate developer in New York City found that the recession was reducing the demand for condominiums in his buildings, so he began offering the empty spaces to local nonprofits, which used them for additional office space. An equipment repair shop next door to a small museum didn't need all its workshop and warehouse space, so it lent part of the space to the museum, which installed its own carpentry shop. These types of loans save nonprofits thousands of dollars a year in facility costs.

Clout

One of the most helpful things you may be able to give your nonprofit partner is clout: that is, your corporate weight applied to its cause. Most nonprofits work hard to effect change in a particular area, but they often lack the contacts or "pull" with officials that can readily promote change. As a business, you may be better positioned to get legislators, other businesses, or community leaders to take action. This works in your interest as well, since once you have adopted a cause, any improvement in that area reflects well on you. As Peter B. Goldberg, former head of the Primerica (Corporation) Foundation, said in talking about how business can further a social agenda, "A corporation can't simply put its money where its mouth is; it's got to put its mouth in the corridors of local, state, and federal governments."

As one part of its Social Responsibility Marketing partnerships program, for example, Easter Seals recruits high-level officers from its corporate partners to sit on its national and local boards. These individuals agree to hire more disabled workers in their businesses, and agree to act as advocates at the community level for disabled children. The clout and example of these corporate leaders add significantly to the impact of Easter Seals' message.

Marketing and Promotion

Your marketing skill is one of the most valuable things you can offer a nonprofit. As we said earlier, the nonprofit's goal is to get its message out to the public: to educate the public and to attract new donors. Since most nonprofits are not experienced marketers, your professional help is extremely valuable.

> Give your nonprofit partner access to your in-house marketing, promotion, and advertising staffs, as well as to your external contractors. Use those people to work on your partner's programs: the better your partner looks, the better you look. Also, young advertising professionals love to work on pro-bono ads. Because of their content, they can be edgier and more creative, and tend to garner a larger share of kudos and awards.

> Involve your partner in developing the promotional aspects of your campaign so that it learns from the experience. Even if they never learn to fly on their own, the smarter they get, the more receptive they'll be to your ideas.

> Include information about your partner in your billing statements or other literature. Mention it in your ads. This cements your relationship in the public mind, and it helps your partner get its message out.

Scott Paper Company offered this kind of assistance to the six charities that received proceeds from the Helping Hand product line. The charities believed this was one of the most beneficial parts of the strategic alliance effort, since it provided continuing benefit after the campaign itself had ended. "Marketing professionals can provide technical assistance that could have a lasting impact on charitable organizations," said Cynthia Giroud, formerly manager of corporate social investment for Scott Paper. "This was one of the major benefits identified by the Helping Hand charities. Working with our advertising agency and marketing group gave them insight into the planning process, the analysis needed for program development, and ways to evaluate the results of their efforts."

Purchasing Goods or Services

You probably purchase a wide range of products and services from a wide range of vendors. Consider adding your partner to your vendor list. For example:

If You Partner an Arts Organization > Can you buy bulk tickets at discount prices to give to employees as perks?

If You Partner a Social Service Agency > Can it offer classes or services for your employees on issues related to its mission, such as crime prevention, substance abuse, or other topics of employee concern?

If You Partner a Health Agency > Can it offer classes or information packets for employees on topics such as weight loss, smoking cessation, stress reduction, or other areas of employee concern?

If You Partner a School, University, or Job Training Program > Can you use its students or trainees as interns?

Think creatively about your partner's business—and about your own needs. You may find more overlap than you first assumed.

Giving Money

Of course, if in addition to all these non-monetary ways to help, you still want to give a nonprofit money (not many will refuse). Here are three things you might consider, in addition to a straight donation:

Low-Interest or No-Interest Loan > Lend the organization money at low or no interest. Take a tax deduction for the interest you're not charging. If the loan is not paid back, it will become a tax-deductible contribution.

Employee Matching Gifts > You'll increase the impact of your donations and please your employees if you offer to match their gifts to nonprofit organizations. This will also be a good way for you to keep tabs on the groups your employees are supporting so that you can be sure to keep your campaign close to their hearts.

Link Your Charitable Giving Program to Organizations in Which Your Employees Volunteer > Many companies give small grants to any nonprofit for which an employee works regularly for six months or longer.

Incorporating Gifts into Your Campaign

Each of these gifts to a nonprofit partner can become an element in your campaign. Each one can be staged as a media event, designed to call attention to your gift and to keep your joint venture in the public eye. In this way they can be used to extend your campaign and keep it fresh.

That doesn't mean that each gift should become a hollow play for publicity—not at all. The insincerity would show and the campaign would backfire. The donations should be genuine responses to needs of the nonprofit, and integral parts of your continuing campaign. They should be indications of your company's continuing commitment to this cause.

To use donations as part of your campaign, first think about what you have to give. Talk to people in different departments to see what corporate resources are being under-used. Make a list of possible donations. Then talk to your partner: ask what it needs, and see if together you can expand the list.

Once you've settled on a list of donations, think about how you want to present each one to get maximum benefit for the cause and for yourself. For instance, if you decide to launch an employee volunteer program, can you launch it with a flourish? Perhaps by staging a media event on the first day of volunteering? Or by inviting the press to view the visible results of the first 100 hours of your employees' time? Not only will the nonprofit benefit from coverage on the evening news, but your employees will feel proud. This may help encourage additional employees to volunteer.

You may want to let your partner run the presentations. They get center stage, and it can dilute or even eliminate some of the mercenary tone. Coming from the recipient, their gracious thanks for a hundred used computers you were going to throw out anyway can sound like "the best gift we've ever gotten, one which will transform our entire organization and bring us into the twenty-first century."

As you plan your campaign to include both marketing events and donation elements, think about the level of "flash" you want each element to have. Some, particularly the marketing events, can be "noisy," full of hype and excitement. Others, particularly the donations, can be "quieter," using feature stories rather than ad campaigns. Some stories can be targeted to special-interest media, others to mass-market outlets. Think about using donations as "spacers" between your marketing events to vary the "pitch" of your campaign and keep the public interested. For instance, after conducting a cause-related marketing campaign that lasts for three months, do some behind-the-scenes giving. Then six months later tell the public what you've been doing, or let it see the results.

By mixing marketing events with donations, you cement your relationship with the nonprofit, maximize your ability to make a difference for its cause, and remind the public of just how committed you are. After all, consumers are buying into your campaign because they support your partner. They want to know that you really support that partner, too. The more ways you can show them, the better.

26

TELLING THE PUBLIC WHAT YOU'RE DOING

"If you did it and you didn't tell anybody... you didn't do it."
— David Ogilvy
Advertising Guru

<   <   <   <

Have you ever said, "I couldn't buy PR like that"?

Now you can. The good news is that joint ventures offer huge areas of media and publicity for your company—the bad news is that they won't succeed without it.

You've crossed over into a different world than your familiar territory of media plans, advertising budgets and rate cards. (Not that you won't still be doing plenty of that.)

In order to make the most of your strategic partnership initiative, you need to plan a publicity campaign that will get you the kind of attention you want. This will be a little different from planning your conventional promotional campaign because with cause-related marketing there are more angles open to you, and you want to take them all.

To craft your public relations plan, work with your nonprofit partner. Your partner's input is critical because they have ideas and contacts you don't have. Together you can explore the wide variety of avenues open to unusual partnerships like yours.

To many of you this chapter may seem obvious and old hat. But you wouldn't believe the number of businesses that engage in cause-related marketing and don't tell anyone they're doing it. We know of ten businesses—no exaggeration—in Seattle alone that have conducted campaigns that nobody knew about. A supermarket chain that gave ten cents to the Nature

Conservancy every time a customer brought their own shopping bag. A coffee retailer that gave four dollars to CARE every time someone bought a gift pack of coffee beans. Restaurants that gave a portion of every meal to local food banks. None of these establishments mentioned their participation anywhere in their stores, or their ads.

Why? We're not sure. Perhaps they felt they were conducting these campaigns out of the goodness of their hearts, purely for the benefit of the nonprofit with no gain for themselves. That's fine—but would their partners benefit any less if consumers knew the campaigns were happening? Of course not! If anything, they would benefit more because consumers would patronize the businesses to support those organizations.

The businesses also missed an opportunity to educate the public about their partners. Couldn't the coffee company benefit CARE more by putting information about the organization in its store? Or in its ads? Or on its bags?

So, please: be as selfless, as non-commercial, as low-key as you like in conducting your campaign. But don't be neglectful. If you don't want to attract money and attention to yourself, at least get them for your nonprofit partner. After all, isn't that why you're doing this?

Getting the Broadest Coverage

Because you are working with a nonprofit on a social issue, you'll have a wider range of media outlets available to you than you ordinarily might. Be systematic in pursuing them so that you get the widest—or most targeted— coverage possible. Once again, you have the ravenous media beast's appetites working in your best interest. If you're newsworthy, you should have no trouble getting onto their menu.

Think About Mass-Market Media > What newspapers, magazines, radio programs, and TV programs might be interested in your campaign? The list will be longer than the one you're used to because of the nature of the campaign. What publications do your target markets read? What do the nonprofit's members read? Read them to get a feel for their stories, then think about how to turn your campaign into a story that interests them.

Think About Targeted Media > Are there special-interest magazines, newsletters, or newspapers that might be interested? What about cable TV stations? What special-interest magazines or television programs do your target markets follow? Your partner's members? How can you make your campaign of interest to them?

Use All Your Partner's Nonprofit Communication Channels > Does it have a Web site, newsletter, or magazine? Does it belong to a nonprofit association that has a newsletter or magazine? Does it have media contacts who like the organization and are likely to take a story? In general, you're better off letting the nonprofit place the stories.

Take Full Advantage of All Your Own Communication Outlets as Well as Those of Your Industry > These include your own Web sites, newsletters or magazines, your billing statements or inserts, industry trade papers, and so on.

Develop Public Service Announcements > PSAs, whether print or broadcast, can be designed to look and feel and draw like any other ads. However, there are restrictions on their placement and content. PSAs must be placed by the nonprofit. They run at the discretion of the station. And they can only advertise the nonprofit activity. Your company can be mentioned as a sponsor of the program, but a PSA can't be an ad for your company, or even for your campaign. For example, if you are partnering a nonprofit in a special event, the PSA can advertise the event, mentioning you as a sponsor. It can't mention your product. Despite these restrictions, PSAs are an excellent way to generate free publicity that benefits your partner and links your name with its name.

Finding New Angles on the Story

Working with a nonprofit also means you have more stories to tell, and more ways to tell them, than you ordinarily would. You may be accustomed to using ads as your primary means of communicating with the public, but in this campaign you can use hard news stories, feature stories, PSAs, and straight ads. You can also tell your campaign story more than one way—to get the greatest amount of coverage. Here are some tips to guide you through story creation and placement:

Think About Which Aspects of Your Joint Venture Are Best Suited to News Stories and Which Are Better Promoted through Ads > Your campaign should have a blend of hard news, feature stories, and ads.

Look for Topical Issues to Which Your Campaign Relates > Has a survey been released on your issue? Has there been a scientific breakthrough in a related area? Has some news story appeared that calls attention to the issue? Use those events as opportunities to plant a story.

Do the Same with Holidays and Special Recognition Periods > Is there a Christmas angle to your campaign? A Mother's Day connection? A special recognition period which your partner knows about? Consider any events relevant to your cause as possible media opportunities.

Look at Your Story from the Point of View of the Media Person You Are Pitching > What will make this story interesting to him or her? Present the story in that light. You ought to be able to sell the same story to *Sports Illustrated* and *Modern Maturity* just by refocusing the lens.

Don't Make Your Company the Focus of the Story > That appears self-serving and will turn off most media. Instead, look for the angle that appeals to that magazine's readers or that program's viewers.

Remember: You Don't Need to Reach Everyone in America or in Your Community > You need only reach the people you and your partner have targeted as your likely customers and supporters. Your audience may be in the millions—or as few as ten thousand. Whatever the size, your goal is to reach your audience as often and in as many ways as possible, so they will hear your message and respond.

Being Clear, or, Expectations Can Kill

It's easy in conducting a media campaign to get caught up in hype. You're excited about what you're doing and you want your excitement to show. But there is a point at which hype turns into dishonesty. Steer clear of it. Don't exaggerate to the public about what the campaign will achieve. Don't suggest a relationship with the nonprofit that doesn't exist. Don't overstep the bounds of common sense and good taste. Doing those things will discredit your CRM venture—and your reputation along with it. (For an example of why you shouldn't do this, see the section on Procter & Gamble and the Arthritis Foundation in chapter 14.)

Work together to develop and implement the publicity campaign. Your partner needs the experience of participating in a promotional campaign. You need your partner's credibility in contacting the media.

Also, both you and your partner are coming to this project with expectations and assumptions the other isn't aware of. When these expectations aren't met, they can sometimes be serious enough to kill the project, often at a very late stage of the process. You both need open and frequent communication to avoid misunderstandings and bad feelings. To avoid problems, follow these guidelines as you plan your media campaign:

Be Clear with Your Partner Ahead of Time and in Writing about What Is Allowable and What Isn't

> What restrictions apply to using your partner's name and logo?

> When can it use yours?

> What information will be included about the nonprofit? Name, address, phone number? Information about the cause? Membership or donation information? Will this be in all campaign promotion or only in selected ads and stories?

> How will you describe the campaign to the public? Agree on wording ahead of time.

> Will partners talk to reporters together or can each partner give interviews alone?

> Do both partners have veto power over ads and PSAs? Will your product names appear in campaign materials?

Be Clear with the Public about How the Money Will Be Raised and Allocated > The public will support your campaign because it believes in the cause. Your supporters will want to know exactly how your partner will benefit. There will be people out there with their own agendas looking for any opportunity to discredit you. Don't give them one.

> Be clear about any limitations on your gift to the nonprofit. Is there a ceiling on your donation? What is it?

> Be honest. Do public purchases really trigger the donation, or will you make the donation regardless? Don't make it look like cause-related marketing if it's really a philanthropic gift.

> Be forthcoming about the results. The public wants to know how well the campaign did. How much money did the nonprofit get? How will it use that money? Several months later, take out ads that tell the public how your partner used the funds. It will be one more chance to remind consumers about how you contributed to the cause.

The Golden Rule

Include your partner in your ads. A nonprofit can't afford to buy the ad space you can. So one of the best ways you can help is by including your partner's message in your ads. Your partner gets its message broadcast. You look like a million dollars.

Communicating the Results

In all the excitement of creating your campaign, don't forget to communicate the results. A common tendency is to put all the effort into the front end of the program and completely ignore the back end. That's bad for a number of reasons:

Customers Want Results > The customers who supported your campaign want to know what it achieved. How much money was collected and where did it go? If you make them feel as if they genuinely helped the cause, they'll be much more likely to participate again next time. Customers also want to know that you did what you said you would. They supported you on faith, in the belief that you would help a cause they cared about. Afterward they want to know that you delivered, so that they know they made a good decision. Keep in mind the Australian consumer poll that basically said public communication was the best way to judge if a company was sincere in its efforts.

Employees Want Results > Your employees were involved in this campaign and they want to know what their efforts accomplished. Even employees who were not actively involved want to know that their employer is really making a difference. The campaign's achievements will make them feel proud.

Your Partner Wants Results > Publicizing the project gives your partner a chance to showcase its accomplishments, and the more accomplished it is, the better able it will be to attract donations.

You Want Results > You want to be able to say, "We made a difference on this issue." Being allowed to publicize the results is one of the best reasons to do cause-related marketing. Don't miss that opportunity!

Publicizing Results Extends Your Campaign > It offers you one last opportunity to grab the spotlight and remind the world about your joint venture. (One of the benefits of long-term or continuing projects is the opportunity to periodically update the results.)

What Do We Mean by Results?

When we say publicize results we don't just mean the amount of money collected during your campaign. As a result of your campaign:

> How many new donors does your partner have?

> How many new volunteers?

> How many more people has it fed? (Or how many more plays has it produced, or how many more people with AIDS has it cared for?)

> What legislation has been proposed to improve the issue?

> What progress has been made on the cause?

Dollars are nice—but abstract in this context. The public wants to help make a difference. It wants to know about tangible results it helped create. That strengthens its connection with the cause and, therefore, with you. Also, in this era of notorious overspending, $1 million may not buy as much as it should. But nobody can argue with the number of children fed, or the number of lives saved.

If you're building a continuing campaign with your partner, create milestones ahead of time, then advertise each time you reach one: the one hundredth new volunteer, the one thousandth adult who learned to read, the first patient to receive a new treatment. Each of these becomes one more way to extend your campaign, and one more way for the public to know that, together, you're making a difference.

27

EVALUATING YOUR CAMPAIGN

"Corporations are going through downsizing and are looking more closely at all of their expenditures and investments. We expect nonprofit organizations to do the same. They need to show us measurements that prove the effectiveness of the programs we fund."

—*Paula Baker*
Vice President
IBM Foundation

<   <   <   <

The following is a true story, but the names have been omitted to protect the inept. In the late 1990s, a local chapter of a national charity decided to mount a fundraising dinner. The society hired a caterer, rented a ballroom, and sent out invitations. It spent $15,000 orchestrating the event. On the appointed night, hundreds of people arrived, wearing furs and smiling warmly. Speeches were made. Pictures were taken. Checks were signed. When the staff retired to their office and counted the money they found they had raised $12,000. "But," said the director, only slightly apologetic, "we got such good PR!"

Before you write this off as silly, unbusinesslike, nonprofit behavior, you should know that a lot of companies do exactly the same thing in evaluating their campaigns. Instead of holding themselves accountable to the marketing goals they established early on, they write off the programs as strictly PR. Why? Not because the programs fail—because the companies fail to take them seriously. Usually, they failed to set comprehensive goals for the programs back at the beginning, so they don't have evaluation criteria when they get to the end.

These companies are missing the boat. Since they don't evaluate their programs, they have no way of knowing how well they performed: where they surpassed expectations, where they fell short, how to improve next time. They don't know how the public perceived the campaigns, or how their employees responded. They can only guess at the programs' impact on sales, at whether they boosted traffic or excited the sales force. And what about the nonprofits? They raised some money—but did they gain any new donors? Any volunteers? Any converts to the cause?

Without evaluation, there's no way to know the answers. Pretty foolhardy, given the amount of money these companies spent. Since they evaluate their other marketing campaigns, why not evaluate this one? As we said, some businesses make some pretty unbusinesslike mistakes. Let's hope your company isn't one of them.

Evaluation by the Goals

Just as there are companies that spend millions of dollars on advertising with only vague notions of real effectiveness, there are cause-related marketing ventures that evaluate their success the same way. It was a success if the President's wife liked it. It was a failure if the CEO didn't have a good time.

Obviously, we don't think that way. Our short evaluation form consists of the following two questions:

1. Did you make money?
2. Did you make a difference?

Like we said, that's the short form. The long form is a little more involved, but worth the effort. Of course, if you've been doing cause-related marketing by the book (this book), you've done the hardest work of evaluation already. You did it back in chapter 18 when you set your goals. You decided at that time what you wanted your program to achieve. Now it's just a matter of learning whether it did.

You'll be evaluating it according to numerous criteria—as many criteria as you included in your goals. Did you have specific sales objectives? You'll have to measure sales results. Did you outline objectives for employee involvement? You'll have to communicate with employees to get their feedback. Did you hope to build awareness of your company in a new geographic market?

You'll have to do market research in that area to find out who noticed. You want to evaluate your campaign the same way you would any conventional sales promotion program—and then tack on a number of other measures, because strategic alliances aren't just a sales promotion.

Depending on your campaign's goals, here are some things you may be looking for:

Sales Results > What was the impact of the campaign on sales volume? On market share? On average purchase quantity and frequency? On brand switching? On trial and repeat purchase behavior? On retail distribution intensity? On coupon redemption or proof-of-purchase returns? On store and warehouse shipments?

Target Market Results > Did heightened sales activity occur in the markets—geographic, socioeconomic, etc.—that you targeted?

Retail Activity > What feedback did you get from retailers, distributors, and franchisees? What did they hear from their customers? What did they read in their local press? What feedback did you get from your sales force? What was the level of retail merchandising activity? What suggestions do these people have for improving future campaigns?

Publicity > How much coverage did you get? Was it where you wanted it? Was it favorable? What will you do differently next time?

Employee Attitudes > Did employees get involved in the campaign? What were their comments? Will they continue to support your partner? What are their thoughts about how the campaign could be improved? What surprised you about employee involvement?

Management Attitudes > Did your managers support the campaign? What are their suggestions for future campaigns?

Public Reaction > How did the public respond to the campaign? Did it respond favorably to your choice of cause and partner? Did your actions seem credible or were they perceived as a marketing gimmick? Did the campaign have an impact on your corporate image? On the image of your products or services? Would the public support an extended campaign on this issue? With this partner? Use market research to find out.

Revenue/Expense Results > What does a cost-benefit analysis tell you about the campaign?

Working Relationship > How was your working relationship with your partner? What would have made it smoother?

Internal Campaign Management > What worked well in the way the campaign was managed? What would have made it smoother?

Ask people at every level for answers to these questions—especially salespeople, retailers, and front-line employees. They were in the best position to see the campaign in action, so make sure you take the opportunity to learn what they learned.

Evaluate the Campaign with Your Partner

Some companies are squeamish about sharing their results with their partners. Don't be. You're not the CIA, and they're not the KGB. This was a joint campaign. You entered it for common gain. Neither could have done it without the other. Now evaluate it together. Learn together what worked and what didn't. If you intend to work together again, this learning is crucial. If you don't, it will help you both work better with other partners in the future.

Here are some things to consider in evaluating your partner's side of the program:

Money > How much money did your partner get? Was it what you had hoped for? What would have increased the take?

Exposure > How much press coverage did your partner get? Was it in the "right" places? Was the "right" message given out?

Public Response > What did the organization hear from its members? From its donors? Did donations increase? Did the organization sign up new members? Did it recruit new volunteers? Did it receive more requests for information? Did the campaign have an impact on its image? On its credibility? How does the general public feel about the organization's participation in the campaign? This information is vital to your nonprofit partner, so vital that it may be worthwhile to pay for market research to find out.

The Cause > What benefits accrued to the cause as a result of the campaign? Did it improve the public's knowledge or awareness of the issue? Again, pay for market research to find out.

Cost-Benefit Analysis > Was the campaign worth doing, given what the opportunity cost?

Working Relationship > How does the organization feel about the partnership? What would have made it smoother? Would it, or will it, work with you again?

Internal Management > How does the organization think the campaign was handled internally? What does it hear from its local chapters? What would have made it smoother?

As with any promotion, it's hard to isolate the effects of one program. Did sales gains and increased volunteer interest really come from this campaign? It's hard to know. The market is shaped by countless forces, so assigning a definitive cause-and-effect is tricky. That's one more reason to think about waging an extended campaign with a long-term partner. That gives the public repeated opportunities to respond and lets you measure results over a longer period. This is especially important in measuring image gains, which accrue gradually. Also, your first campaign may not turn out to be everything you hoped. Some campaigns are more successful than others, even for the pros. American Express raised $4 million for local charities with its Project Hometown America campaign—but card use and new card purchases increased only marginally. Overall, though, the company's numerous cause-related marketing campaigns have contributed greatly to both the business results and the image of the company. So amortize your risks and increase your opportunities for gain by making strategic alliances an integral part of your operation.

28

PUTTING IT ALL TOGETHER: A HYPOTHETICAL CAMPAIGN

"Do what you can, with what you have, where you are."
                                        — *Theodore Roosevelt*

<   <   <   <

What does a multi-layered campaign look like in practice? Let's put one together so that you can see the thinking from start to finish. Then we'll pull it apart, to find out what worked and what didn't. There's a lot to be learned from bad examples, especially in cause-related marketing, where many companies make the same mistakes.

For the purpose of this example, let's create a small chain of upscale grocery stores called Bob's Basket. You've been in stores like Bob's. The produce counter displays seven types of lettuce. The shelves stock Dijon mustard but not French's. The butchers wear red-and-white-checked aprons and name tags. The store's monthly newsletter features environmentally friendly products and recipes using sun-dried tomatoes and shitaake mushrooms. Bob's hallmarks are quality, service, and premium prices.

Let's also give Bob's some background and some marketing goals. The chain opened in Los Angeles in 1990 and quickly spread to San Francisco, San Jose, and Sacramento. By 1994 it had opened stores in Portland, Seattle, and Chicago. By 1996 it was preparing its East Coast launch. In each city, the stores were located in thriving retail areas near, but not in, downtown; their target market was the young-to-middle-aged professionals who lived and worked in those neighborhoods. Despite a lot of competition in the upscale grocery market, Bob's Basket was a strong player in every city, with a healthy share of the market.

Now, as the company planned its East Coast launch, managers contemplated adding a strategic partnership element to their marketing efforts. Supporting a social cause would fit with the personal beliefs of the store's owners and employees. It would appeal to the clientele, and it could become an integral part of Bob's image as the chain became a national entity. Over the years, the company had dabbled in philanthropy, giving small amounts to a variety of causes, but had never thought strategically about those donations. Its campaign would require starting from square one. What social issue should it pick? What nonprofit organization? What should be the elements of the campaign? Store managers weighed the possibilities.

Everyone decided quickly that whatever cause they picked, the campaign should be long-term. Durability would indicate the company's sincerity: "It shouldn't just look like a marketing gimmick," they agreed. Durability would also strongly identify the company with the issue. "We want customers to think, 'Bob's: the store that cares about X,' when they think of us," said one of the marketing managers, and that became the goal of the campaign.

They also quickly decided to target "the hungry" as a campaign theme: they believed that customers who were buying food for themselves would respond to the chance to help others in need. The choice of a nonprofit was a little tougher: should they go local, partnering a food bank in each city? No. Now that the company was national, they believed they needed a national partner. But none of the national agencies they could think of had the instant name recognition and image of quality they wanted associated with the stores. Ultimately, they settled on CARE, an international food distribution agency with a long history and a well-established reputation. Bob's managers felt comfortable with those traits, and believed their customers would respond.

Their next decision was how to structure the campaign. They liked the idea of a cause-related marketing scheme—helping the cause and their sales at the same time. So they decided that for every $25 purchase, they would give one dollar to CARE. The campaign would go on indefinitely, as a sign of the company's serious commitment, and would be advertised in print ads and point-of-purchase displays. They decided to print a message about CARE on their grocery bags and to put leaflets about the organization at every cash register. These strategies, they thought, would make their commitment apparent and credible, and an integral part of the business. To kick off the campaign they held a press conference at which they presented CARE with a check for

$5,000. The story appeared on the business page of the local paper in most of their cities.

Campaign Results from Hunger

Unfortunately, the campaign didn't pan out the way Bob's managers had anticipated. Consumers just didn't respond in a big way. Oh, they were sympathetic. Clerks got positive comments about the program and shoppers were happy their purchases were helping CARE. But the program had no noticeable effect on sales. Despite the large advertising campaign, traffic figures held steady. Despite the point-of-purchase displays, sales figures showed no appreciable gain. After several months, Bob's ran discount coupons in local papers, hoping to increase response. The coupons offered a discount on selected products which would trigger an additional donation to CARE. Customers redeemed the coupons—but at the typical redemption rate. The CARE connection didn't have a measurable impact.

After a year of tinkering with the program, managers decided to call it quits. The program wasn't working and they didn't know why. Maybe the grocery business wasn't designed for strategic partnerships. Maybe customers were tired of the cause-related approach. Certainly the marketing managers were tired of it, and had better things to do besides. The first East Coast store had opened and was demanding their attention. Almost a year to the day from the date of the press conference, Bob's quietly ended its campaign. Managers say maybe one day they'll try again: they like the idea of helping a social cause while boosting sales. The employees seemed to like it. But for some reason, this time it just didn't seem to work.

Why Did Bob's Campaign Fall Flat?

What was the problem with Bob's campaign? Is it true that the grocery business can't support strategic alliances? Or that customers are tired of helping a worthy cause? Hardly. The problem with Bob's campaign was that it was poorly conceived. Bob's managers took a great idea and ruined it with a couple of poor decisions. Let's dissect the campaign and find out why. Then let's reconstruct it to make it work.

Goals

Bob's managers made a critical mistake right up front. They failed to delineate their goals. Whom did they want to reach: what income group? what geographic group? What did they want to achieve: new business? repeat business? Campaigns should support specific goals—not just generate warm, fuzzy feelings. Had Bob's managers planned theirs strategically, they could have designed a campaign that worked. As it was, they were doomed to fail because they didn't know where they were going. Had the managers looked through their marketing, philanthropic, and human resource goals, they might have come up with a list like this:

1. **Business Goals >** The campaign should:
   > increase customer loyalty to our stores. We want to become our customers' regular supermarket.
   > woo customers from the competition. We want to attract upscale, urban professionals and residents.
   > increase walk-in traffic in each store. We want to encourage new people to try our stores.
   > encourage people to spend more money in the stores.

2. **Image Goals >** The campaign should:
   > strengthen each store's image as "the neighborhood store."
   > reinforce the company's image of quality and service.
   > show that Bob's cares about its community, not just about profits.

3. **Social Goals >** The campaign should:
   > have a demonstrable effect on a social problem of concern to our customers.

4. **Employee Goals >** The campaign should:
   > enable employees to participate in a social cause through volunteering.
   > give employees the feeling that they can help make a difference on a social problem.
   > build employees' loyalty to the company.

5. **Exposure** > The campaign should:
> be unusual and mediagenic in order to attract media attention in each local market.
> attract at least one feature story in every local paper and, if possible, a mention on the local evening news.

Choice of Issue

Hunger and food store: a good match or a forced connection? Good match. Bob's managers played it right on this one. There is a tight and logical fit between the issue and the business. They were right to think their customers would respond to a chance to feed the needy while stocking up themselves. But they were lucky. They should have checked this out with market research. Relying on instinct can be dangerous in picking an issue because you're apt to choose your own preference, rather than your customers'.

Choice of Partner

Who cares about CARE? Lots of people do—and thank goodness they send checks. But did CARE's demographics match up with Bob's customers? The majority of people on the streets of Los Angeles, Chicago, or New York care more about the people they step over every day as they walk into Bob's stores—the hungry and homeless in their own backyards. Those people are a major problem to them: one they wish they didn't encounter daily, one they wish they could do something about. Bob's had a chance to address that concern—but passed on the opportunity. Instead Bob's picked a partner that was worthy—but invisible. CARE is a great choice as a philanthropy recipient—but for a marketing partner, it's weak.

Bob's broke one of the most fundamental rules of cause-related marketing: match the geography of your partner to the geography of your markets. The company needed a local campaign, not a national one, and certainly not one that is perceived by the general public as helping primarily the Third World. The managers wanted to strengthen each store's ties to its neighborhood, not remind their customers they were shopping at a national chain. A local partner would have tugged much more directly at customers' heartstrings. It would also have offered concrete opportunities for getting employees, customers, and the press involved.

The logical partner would have been a food bank or homeless shelter in each city with a Bob's store. Again, market research—even just informal polling of customers and prospective customers—would have helped Bob's make an effective choice. Unfortunately, Bob's marketers—who routinely use research in designing their sales campaigns—put their good sense aside and became philanthropists with their marketing program.

Developing the Campaign

Suppose Bob's had done market research and had picked a local homeless shelter in every city with a store. Now what? What should the campaign include? Bob's selected some good elements: a cause-related marketing campaign, information on the bags, a generous donation.

What went wrong? Not much—but more things could have gone right. Had Bob's probed its business areas more thoroughly, it could have come up with other campaign elements that might have generated more interest and enthusiasm from customers and the media. Bob's could have tied the campaign to its goals in a much more powerful way. For instance, had Bob's managers looked at more options and brainstormed possibilities in each, they might have come up with a list like this:

Strategic Philanthropy

What could Bob's do here?

The stores could give each shelter a $1,000 donation. For $2,000 more than the $5,000 gift to CARE, they could have made a significant contribution in each of their seven cities.

Cause-Related Marketing

What could Bob's do here? Several things:

> Twenty-five cents per bag: In the CARE campaign, Bob's gave one dollar to CARE for every $25 purchase. A nice gesture. Doesn't do much for people who spend less than $25, though. And it doesn't do much for walk-in traffic, which Bob's was trying to encourage. A better strategy would be to donate twenty-five cents to the shelter for every bag of groceries purchased. Decreasing the size of the purchase

would make it easier for shoppers to contribute. It would enable walk-ins to participate, since they are unlikely to spend $25. And it would have little impact on Bob's overall donation.

> "Bob's Coupons": Had the managers probed a little further, they might have come up with a second cause-related marketing strategy. For every bag of groceries purchased, customers could choose to get a Bob's Coupon, good for a free meal at the local homeless shelter, which they could give out to panhandlers. The coupon would support the campaign's goals in two ways. One, it would encourage homeless people to use the shelters, giving them more help than a handout. Two, it would increase customer's involvement in the program, turning a blind, one-step action (donating money) into a two-step, empowering process (getting the coupon by shopping at Bob's, then helping a homeless person directly). Three, it would give customers who feel uncomfortable when approached by a street person an easy, positive response.

Special Events

What could Bob's do here? Again, several things:

> A contest: The chain could hold a month-long contest among Bob's stores to see which store could generate the biggest donation to its local shelter. This would build customer loyalty to the neighborhood store, encourage repeat business, and serve Bob's marketing goal of encouraging customers to see Bob's as their regular grocery store. It would also activate employee involvement, encouraging them to increase customer activity in the spirit of friendly competition.

> Holiday events: Bob's could hold special holiday events designed to trigger additional donations. For instance: at Thanksgiving they could offer to make an additional donation to the shelter for every turkey bought. They could donate a turkey to the shelter for every 100 turkeys sold. They could give each turkey-buying customer a number so that the customer would feel they were contributing.

> Family events: To build business with families, Bob's could hold "family days" at the stores, with specials on children's food items, cooking demonstrations geared to kids, easy-to-make recipes on cards, etc. Children who brought donations of non-perishable food items would trigger an additional donation to the shelter.

Premiums

What could Bob's do here? While we've seen examples of premiums produced by the homeless in shelters, it takes more work than makes sense for Bob's. Let's move on to the next strategic alliance option.

Licensing

What could Bob's do here? Again, not much. Licensing a homeless shelter doesn't lend itself to a venture with Bob's, either. Let's keep going.

Sponsored Ads

Bingo. There's lots that Bob's could do here:

> Add a message to their ads: They could include a message about homelessness in each of their ads, designed to educate the public about the issue.

> Advertise success: They could take out ads to advertise milestones in their campaign. For example: the day that Bob's and its customers fed the one thousandth person at the shelter, the day that Bob's and its customers donated $100,000 through their cause-related marketing campaign, the day that Bob's and its customers donated $1 million worth of food. These milestones would let the public and the customers know the campaign was working.

> In-store advertising: Bob's could place educational messages about homelessness on its grocery bags and on in-store displays. The store could put articles about people who work and stay at the shelter in the company newsletter and on the bulletin board.

> Slogan: Bob's could develop a campaign slogan, such as "Help Bob's Help the Homeless." The slogan could appear on everything: aprons, grocery bags, signs, trucks. Everywhere it appeared there would be a short message educating the public about the issue—and reminding customers about Bob's commitment to the cause.

Vendor Relationships

What could Bob's do here? How about hire people from the shelter for day jobs: gathering shopping carts, guiding cars in the parking lot? There are labor issues to consider: because of union regulations or seniority issues this may not be possible. Some groups that have hired the homeless at lower than the minimum wage have even been accused of unethical business practices. But it's worth investigating. There are companies that have succeeded in this area. Hiring people from the shelter could enable Bob's to help its adopted cause in a very direct way.

Employee Volunteers

What could Bob's do here? Again, lots:

> Encourage volunteering: At the very least, Bob's could encourage its employees to volunteer at the shelter. To support a volunteer campaign, it could print stories about volunteers in the company newsletter and post them on each store's bulletin board. Volunteers could get special name tags to further increase recognition. The tags could even say, "Ask Me About Volunteering" to incite customer curiosity and open opportunities for customer involvement as well.

> "Bob's Night" : The stores could also hold an annual or semiannual "Bob's Night" at the shelter, when all store employees (wearing Bob's aprons) would cook and serve dinner using food donated by Bob's.

In-Kind Donations

What could Bob's do here?

> Food donations: Each Bob's store could donate all its less-than-fresh

food to the local shelter. Not only is this tax-deductible, but it reinforces Bob's message that it sells only the best.

> Customer donations: Bob's could encourage its customers to support the shelter by placing a barrel for customer's donations of canned and packaged goods in each store.

> "Bob's Coupons": In addition to giving a "Bob's Coupon" with purchases, Bob's could sell Bob's Coupons at each cash register for twenty-five cents so that customers could buy as many as they wish and hand them out to homeless people on the street. Bob's would support the free meals by donating food to the shelter.

Media Exposure

How could Bob's generate media interest? It shouldn't be too difficult. The unusual nature of some of these events would attract the press. Bob's would just need to be systematic in calling attention to them. Imagine, for instance, the visual impact of all Bob's employees, wearing Bob's aprons, cooking and serving at the local shelter. Or the donation of hundreds of turkeys the day before Thanksgiving—a donation made possible by Bob's customers. Or the story of the one thousandth person fed thanks to Bob's customers' patronage. These are the kinds of positive stories the media like to cover. They are tailor-made for closing bits on the local evening news, and for feature pieces in the "life-style" section of the local paper.

Rolling Out the Campaign

Each of these elements could be rolled out sequentially to create a long-term campaign. The program might kick off with the cash donations, followed by the continuing cause-related marketing campaign. Sponsored ads would announce the campaign to the public. Several months later, Bob's might introduce another element, say "Family Days" or holiday events. Again, several months later the stores could hold "Bob's Night" at the shelter. After a pause of several more months, a series of sponsored ads might announce campaign milestones or tell stories about employee volunteers. By staggering the events and publicizing each one, Bob's could easily keep this campaign going for years. Of course, the stores should monitor customer response through sales and traffic data and through questionnaires. And they should adjust the campaign in response to what they learn.

All of these elements are strategically designed to meet Bob's specific marketing, philanthropy, and human resource goals. But they also have other benefits. They give each store—managers and employees—a sense of autonomy within the campaign. They help Bob's customers deal concretely with a problem they encounter every day. By working the social issue into many facets of Bob's business, they enable the company to have a real impact on the problem. Unlike the poorly conceived campaign Bob's managers came up with, this campaign should work.

General Rules for Strategic Alliances

That's it. We're just about done. Before we go, we wanted to leave you with a few general rules for creating your joint venture:

> For a joint venture to succeed, your company must be committed to the strategy from senior management down.

> Use market research to select your cause and your partners and to develop your program elements.

> Make sure there is a logical association among your cause, your partner, and your product or service.

> Make sure there is a match among your target markets, your partner's constituency, and the geographic reach of your program.

> Develop a good working relationship with your partner by emphasizing open communication and contractual agreements.

> Commit sufficient resources, attention, and priority to your program.

> Be committed to your cause: its gain is your gain. The public will sense insincerity.

> Be up-front about the financial and social benefits of your partnership.

> And last of all, never forget why you're doing it in the first place. This isn't about altruism, it's about... *making money while making a difference!*

(Well, what did you think we were going to say?)

29

CONCLUSION

This is not going to be a long-winded conclusion.

You've just seen examples of companies big and small that have increased sales, attracted new customers, and inspired consumer loyalty through strategic alliances. You've seen the many different opportunities strategic alliances offer a corporation. You've even learned how to plan a strategic alliance initiative for your company. You've also seen the great, important, meaningful impact that joint ventures can have.

So...

It's time to get serious.

Business has always gotten a bad rap. If you're passionate about your job, you get called greedy, or selfish, or misguided. Profits are ugly, horrible, evil goals, to be mentioned in whispers, only bragged about by the greedy fat cats over cigars and brandy while they plot to rule the world.

Hell, you probably said it once or twice yourself when you were younger.

Are you ready to hear the truth?

Business can be bad, but it can also be good.

The choice is almost always up to the people who do business.

In other words, the choice is up to you.

What are you going to do about it?

>   >   <   <

Articles

Abshire, M. "The Kids Are Alright." *Corporate Philanthropy Report* 12, 8 (August 1997): 1, 4–6.

Andreasen, A. "Profits for Nonprofits: Find a Corporate Partner." *Harvard Business Review* 74, 6 (November-December 1996): 47–59.

Aschermann, Kurt. "10 Commandments of Cause-Related Marketing." *Corporate Philanthropy Report* 12, 8 (August 1997): 5.

Burke, E. "Forget the Government. It's the Community that Can Shut You Down." *Business Ethics* 11, 3 (May-June 1997): 11–15.

Carter, M. "Charities Opt for Brand Aid." *The Independent on Sunday* (September 17, 1995).

Collins, J. "The Foundation for Doing Good (The Long View)." *Inc.* (December 1997): 41–42.

Davidson, J. "Cancer Sells." *Working Woman* (May 1997): 36–39, 68.

Dees, G.J. "Enterprising Nonprofits." *Harvard Business Review* 76, 1 (January-February 1998): 55–67.

Dodson, L. "Business to the Rescue." *The Australian Financial Review* (May 19, 1998): 18.

"Filter Queen Builds Trustworthy Partnership." (Case Study) *Corporate Philanthropy Report* 13, 6. (June 1998): 3.

"Forecasts." *Corporate Philanthropy Report* 12, 3. (March 1997): 12.

"Forecasts." *Corporate Philanthropy Report* 13, 10. (October 1998): 12.

Friedman, S. "Charity, Know Thy Corporate Partner—and Thyself." *The Chronicle of Philanthropy.* (October 30, 1997).

Gray, R. "Cause for Thought." *Marketing* (January 2, 1997): 20–21.

Harrison, B. "Bringing High Tech to Low-Income People." (MIT Technology Review), *MIT Alumni Magazine* (April 6, 1997) (Reprint): 64.

"Independent Eye on Cause-Related Marketing, An." (Special Report Insert) *The*

Independent. (November 11, 1998): 1–8.

Kadlec, D. "Business." *Time* (May 5, 1997): 63–64.

Klein, M. "The Burden of Longevity." *Corporate Philanthropy Report* 11, 1 (December 1995): 1, 4–6.

Lang, L. "Human Services Thrive on Pioneer Spirit." *Puget Sound Business Journal—Corporate Citizenship: A Special Report* (June 7–13, 1996) (Reprint): 18A.

"LensCrafters Program Energizes Employees." (Case Study) *Corporate Philanthropy Report* 13, 10. (October 1998): 3, 7.

Martin, Nita. "Deciding What Is Important." *Corporate Philanthropy Report* 12, 3, 1 (March 1997): 3–6.

McCarrell, P. (1998, February 27–March 12). "Nonprofit Buys Redmond Printing Firm." *Eastside Business Journal* 4, 3 (February 27–March 12, 1998) (Reprint).

McLeod, H. "The New Social Entrepreneurs." *Who Cares* (April 1997): 30–34.

McLeod, H. "Crossover: The Social Entrepreneur." *Inc. (Special Issue): The State of Small Business 1997* (1997): 100–105.

Mulhair, G. "Public/Private Partnerships Create New Jobs." *Puget Sound Business Journal* 18, 30 (December 5–11, 1997). (Reprint).

Neill, N. "The Corporate Connection." *Explore* (August-September 1995): 29–33.

"Philanthropy In America: The Gospel of Wealth." (May 30, 1998) *The Economist*: 19–21.

"Pledges From Businesses and Charities to Help Meet Summit's Goals." *The Chronicle of Philanthropy.* (May 29, 1997): 33–35.

Ramsey, B. "This Company Hires People Others Shun—And It Works." *Seattle Post-Intelligencer* (March 25, 1998). (Reprint).

Ratnesar, R. "Doing Well by Doing Good: Bottom-Line Charity." The New Republic. (January 6, 1997).

Prinzing, D. "Pioneer Spirit." *Puget Sound Business Journal* (Small Business Weekly). 18, 27 (November 14–20, 1997). (Reprint): 16–17.

Reinhard, B. "You've Got to Have Heart." *Corporate Philanthropy Report* 12, 4. (April 1997): 1, 4–5.

Salazar, G. "Connecting Commerce with Communities: Cause-Related Marketing Handbook for Corporate & Nonprofit Partners." *Capstone Project Report* presented to the faculty of University College, University of Denver. (May 25, 1997).

Savelle, J. "Property Manager Learned the Hard Way." *Seattle Daily Journal of Commerce.* (December 5, 1997). (Reprint).

"Scuttlebut." *Corporate Philanthropy Report* 13, 10. (October 1998): 2.

Smith, Carol. "Quality Products Both Industrial and Human." *Seattle Post-Intelligencer.* (December 27, 1996). (Reprint).

Smith, Craig. "The Emerging Paradigm." *Corporate Philanthropy Report* 9, 9. (June 1994): 1, 3–6.

Smith, C. "Corporate Giving Officers Prove their Worth." *Corporate Philanthropy Report* 9, 11. (August 1994): 1, 3–4.

"Spotlight: Consumer Products." *Corporate Philanthropy Report* 13, 6. (June 1998): 6–10.

Steckel, R. & Lehman, J. "Building a Corporate Partnership." *The NonProfit Times.* (October 1993): 34–35.

Steckel, R. & Lehman, J. "Making The Case." *The NonProfit Times.* (August 1994): 36.

Steckel, R. & Lehman, J. "The Ultimate Network." *The NonProfit Times.* (October 1994): 39.

Steckel, R. & Lehman, J. "Public Purpose Marketing." *The NonProfit Times.* (April 1995): 29–30.

Stehle, V. "A Charity that Earns Its Way." *The Chronicle of Philanthropy.* (May 3, 1994). (Reprint).

Willson, J. "Good Cause Applause." (Media & Marketing). *The Herald Sun.* (June 11, 1997).

Worcester, A. "Firm Helps Put Lives Back on Track." *West Seattle Herald* 81, 5. (January 29, 1997). (Reprint).

Yankey, J. "A Marriage of Necessity." *Advancing Philanthropy.* (National Society of Fund Raising Executives). (Winter 1996–97): 11–18.

Books

Brown, Peter C. *The Complete Guide to Money Making Ventures for Nonprofit Organizations.* Washington, D.C.: The Taft Group, 1986.

Bryce, Herrington J. *Financial & Strategic Management for Nonprofit Organizations.* Englewood Cliffs, New Jersey: Prentice-Hall, 1987.

Gingold, Diane J. Strategic *Philanthropy in the 1990s: Handbook of Corporate Development Strategies for Nonprofit Managers.* Washington, D.C.: Diane Gingold & Associates, 1993.

Kotler, Philip, and Alan Andreasen. *Strategic Marketing for Nonprofit Organizations.* Englewood Cliffs, New Jersey: Prentice-Hall, 1995.

Shannon, James P. *The Corporate Contributions Handbook: Devoting Private Means to Public Needs.* San Francisco: Jossey-Bass Publishers, 1991.

Steckel, Richard, Robin Simons, and Peter Lengsfelder. *Filthy Rich and Other*

Nonprofit Fantasies: Changing the Way Nonprofits Do Business in the '90s. Berkeley, California: Ten Speed Press, 1989.

Steckel, Richard, and Jennifer Lehman. *In Search of America's Best Nonprofits.* San Francisco: Jossey-Bass Publishers, 1997.

Stepping Out Into the Marketplace: The Pitfalls of Earned Income for the Small Nonprofits. New York: Community Resource Exchange, 1986.

Reports

Adkins, S., and R. McNeil. *Cause-Related Marketing Corporate Survey Report* London: Business in the Community, 1996.

Adkins, S., and V. Murfin. *The Winning Game: Cause-Related Marketing Consumer Research.* London: Business in the Community., 1996.

Adkins, S. *The Game Plan: Cause-Related Marketing Qualitative Consumer Research* (executive summary). London: Business in the Community, 1997.

Adkins, S. *The Cause-Related Marketing Guidelines: Towards Excellence.* London: Business in the Community, 1998.

Alperson, M. *Corporate Giving Strategies that Add Business Value: A Research Report* (Report No. 1126-95-HR). New York: The Conference Board, 1995.

Ben & Jerry's Homemade Inc. *1997 Social Report.* Waterbury, Vermont: Ben & Jerry's Homemade Inc., 1997.

Cavill & Co./Worthington DiMarzio. *The New Bottom Line: Directions for Cause Related Marketing in Australia.* Cavill & Co./Worthington DiMarzio, 1997.

Cone Inc. *New National Survey Documents Consumer Response to Breast Cancer Awareness Month* (press release). Cone Inc.: November 5, 1998.

GrandMetropolitan. *Report on Corporate Citizenship.* London: Grand-Metropolitan, 1997.

Logan, D. *Companies in Communities: Getting the Measure.* London: The London Benchmarking Group, 1997.

Logan, D., D. Roy, and L. Regelbrugge. *Global Corporate Citizenship Rationale and Strategies.* Washington, D.C.: The Hitachi Foundation, 1997.

Pioneer Human Services. *Program Overview* (press kit). Pioneer Human Services, June 1998.

Prima Europe. *Community Affairs Briefing Issue,* No. 30. London: Prima Europe, October 1996.

Working Assets. *Working Assets Guide To Services* (brochure). San Francisco: Working Assets, January 1998.

World Wildlife Fund for Nature (WWF). *Corporate Relationships* (brochure). World Wildlife Fund.

Internet / Online Sources

American Express. (1999). (Web site). http://americanexpress.com.

Bauder, D. "Talk show host wages war with mouthwash." Associated Press. (Available online article). *The Daily Iowan*. (March 21, 1997). http://www.uiowa.edu/~dlyiowan/issue/v128/i164/stories.

Better Business Bureau, the. *Philanthropic Advisory Service Report: Gifts In Kind International*. (1999). (Web site). http://www.bbb.org/reports/charity.html.

Better Business Bureau, the. *Philanthropic Advisory Service Report: National Association For The Exchange Of Industrial Resources*. (1999). (Web site). http://www.bbb.org/reports/charity.html.

Body Shop, the. (1999). (Web site). http://www.the-body-shop.com.

Boys & Girls Clubs of America. (1998). (Web site). http://www.bgca.org.

Clinton, Bill. (January 19, 1999) State of the Union Address. (Online transcript). http://www.cnn.com/ALLPOLITICS/stories/1999/01/19/sotu.transcript/

Electronic Data Systems. (1999). (Web site). http://www.eds.com.

For All Kids Foundation Inc., the. (1998). (Web site). http://rosieo.warnerbros.com/cmp/allkids/allkids.htm.

Hole in the Wall Gang Camp, the. (1999). (Web site). http://www.holeinthewall-gang.org.

Home Depot. (1995). *Painting Our World Orange: The Home Depot Social Responsibility Report 1995* (Web site). http://www.homedepot.com.

Newman's Own Inc. (1998). (Web site). http://www.newmansown.com.

New York Cares. (1999). (Web site). http://nycares.com.

Norwich Union Group. (1998). (Web site). http://www.norwich-union.co.uk.

Sainsbury's. (1999). (Web site). http://www.sainsburys.co.uk.

Salaman, L. (1997). *Holding the Center: America's Nonprofit Sector at a Crossroads*. (Web site). The Nathan Cummings Foundation. http://www.ncf.org.

Second Harvest. (1999). (Web site). http://www.secondharvest.org.

Share Our Strength. (1999). (Web site). http://www.strength.org.

Social Investment Forum. (November 5, 1997). *1997 Report on Responsible Investing Trends in the United States*. (Web site). http://www.socialinvest.org.

Social Investment Forum. (December 5, 1996). *Report: "King Tobacco" May Be Dethroned for Big Investors in 1997*. (Press Release) (Web site). http://www.socialinvest.org.

Target Stores/Dayton Hudson Corporation. (1999). (Web site). http://www.dhc.com.

Tesco. (1999). (Web site). http://www.tesco.co.uk/indexn.htm.

Timberland Company. (1999). (Web site). http://www.timberland.com.

Working Assets Long Distance. (1998). (Website). http://www.wald.com.

ABOUT THE AUTHORS

Richard Steckel, the president and founder of AddVenture Network in Denver, has an international reputation as a consultant and speaker on nonprofit marketing and for-profit cause-related marketing.

Before founding AddVenture Network in 1984, he was the executive director of the Denver Children's Museum, which became a national model of the earned income approach to fundraising.

Dr. Steckel has worked extensively with many corporations and nonprofits in the U.S., Great Britain, Australia, and New Zealand.

Since 1984, Dr. Steckel has developed earned income strategies and products and services for more than one hundred nonprofit and for-profit organizations. He is the author of the widely-read book, *Filthy Rich & Other Nonprofit Fantasies* and *In Search of America's Best Nonprofits*.

Prior to his tenure at the Denver Children's Museum, Dr. Steckel was director of international programs for a Boston-based technical assistance organization, an adult educator, and a community organizer on New York City's Lower East Side. He holds a Ph.D. from Boston University (1974) and a Master's degree in Social Work (Community Organization) from Adelphi University (1966).

Dr. Steckel lives in Denver, Colorado.

Robin Simons has authored seven books, including *The Couple Who Became Each Other* (with David Calof), *After the Tears: Parents Talk About Rasing a Child with a Disability*, and *Filthy Rich & Other Nonprofit Fantasies* (with Richard Steckel).

Before becoming a writer, Ms. Simons worked for many years in the museum field, at the Boston and Denver Chidren's Museums, as a consultant in museum programming and interactive exhibit design, and as a consultant to the National Endowment for the Arts. She has a Master's in Teaching from Leslie College and a Bachelor of Arts with a major in Art History from Brandeis University.

She lives with her daughter and husband on Bainbridge Island, Washington.

Jeffrey Simons (no relation to Robin), after a decade in advertising that included running his own agency and serving on the board of directors of AdNet, one of New York's premier public service advertising groups, left to write books and make games. Mr. Simons is currently CEO of Q.E.D. Games Inc., makers of historical, satirical, and educational games that include "Context 2000: The Learning Game for the Next Milennium." *Making Money While Making a Difference* is Mr. Simons' first work of non-fiction; other works include *Lexicon: Words and Images of Strange* and *When Spirits Come In On the Wind.*

Norman Tanen, in addition to collaborating on this book, is also a workshop trainer and strategic counselor to ad agencies and marketing companies. As he puts it, "I see myself as Jiminy Cricket, whispering into people's ears about how their business lives can be simpler, more productive, and more in alignment with their fellow workers."

He's perfectly suited to that role because, for the thirty years prior to setting up his training company, The Woods Group, Mr. Tanen worked as a senior creative person in some of the largest advertising agencies in the world, experiencing complicated, unproductive, and misaligned relationships.

Over the years, Mr. Tanen has satisfied his public purpose interests by creating a pro-bono group to service The Coalition for the Homeless, helping found an industry advocacy group call AdNet, and establishing educational programs while he was president of The One Club, the definitive group for art directors and copywriters. He is currently involved with a major expansion program of the ninety-year-old Mark Twain Library in his hometown of Redding, Connecticut.

Mr. Tanen is the father of four sons and a husband of one wife (currently). "I am indeed fortunate," he says, "to have a wife like Ilene who allows me to follow my passions."

A NOTE ON THE TYPE

The text of this book was set in Electra, a typeface designed in 1935 by the renowned designer and illustrator William A. Dwiggins (1880-1956). A standard book typeface since its release due to the evenness of design and high legibility, this face cannot be classified as either modern or old style. It is not based on any historical model, nor does it echo any particular period or style. It avoids the extreme contrasts between thick and thin elements that mark most modern faces, and it gives a feeling of fluidity, warmth, personality, and speed.

Printed and bound by McNaughton & Gunn Inc.,
Saline, Michigan

Cover design by June Fernandez
Book design by Alex Lubertozzi